The Bloo Fath

Reclaiming Masculinity through the Wisdom of
Warrior Cultures and General Badasses

by

Wallace Smedley

THE BLOOD OF OUR FATHERS

DEDICATION

Figure 1: CJ Macadaeg August 13, 1992 - October 19, 2017

This book is dedicated to the memory of Christian Jordan (CJ) Macadaeg, my only son. Taken from us too soon, at only twenty-six years old. There has not been a single day yet where I have not wished it was me instead of him who had to go, and I cannot find meaning in this unnatural order.

Lighthearted and quick to laugh at almost anything, to everyone who knew him, he was bigger than life. An incredible mind paired with a cutting wit made him impossible to one-up. His absence leave a hole in our hearts that cannot be filled.

I hope he is proud of this work, as I was of the Man he became.

Contents

ACKNOWLEDGMENTS

Any list of people who were helpful or influential in the creation of this book would be incomplete. The greatest debt is owed to the many warrior cultures, and the warriors therein who fought and lived and died as real men, leaving behind an example for us to see what men are truly capable of accomplishing when we are not fettered by outside forces telling us that we are responsible for all of the wrongs in the world. To them, I bow and give thanks.

What this book is:

In a neighborhood park, the children are playing. One boy is playing that he is Batman. He has a cape and cowl made by his Mother, or perhaps his Grandmother, and he is completely carefree, yet totally serious as he wraps the cape around his arm and runs, the rest of the cape flowing freely behind him. He is having fun and playing the hero.

Another group of boys is playing war. They have pieces of fallen branches, broken into shapes to resemble guns. They excitedly pretend to shoot at one another, and occasionally, one of the boys will fall down "dead."

On the basketball court, boys are playing with teams made up of whoever was there. They are competitive and trying fiercely to outplay the other team, although there is no trophy or real glory on the line, they are playing for personal pride. Their sheer aggression hides the fact that all of them are friends with one another.

This is what boys do when you leave them alone. They learn through play about the different aspects of being a man. They learn to be a hero, to be brave, and to compete. Competition itself teaches them about winning and losing and how to handle either in such a way as to maintain their dignity. Throughout the animal kingdom one will find similar behavior in the male of any species. When we let nature take its course, we will find that the boys do not need to have the do-gooders hovering at every moment in an absurd attempt to prevent any hurt feelings or sense of inadequacy.

And they certainly do not need to be told that traits such as competitiveness, heroic thoughts, and fighting for a just cause are bad things.

There are those in our day who would look at the boys playing and feel the need to fret about the *toxic* aspects of masculinity that the boys are learning through these games. The play will be twisted into excuses for hand-wringing worries about potential future violent behavior, and how *someone* must do *something* to prevent this from happening.

This book is a Father's response to the nonstop assault on everything manly in our world. If this idea offends you, put this book down and walk away slowly, and avert your eyes while you do so, lest the toxic masculinity contained herein contaminate your delicate sensibilities.

For those still here, thank you. You are the reason I still have hope that the male nature will survive the assault, and even thrive in response. We men are no strangers to adversity and hate, in many ways we are born for it, we exist to stand up in conflict and face our enemies, or die in the trying.

For many thousands of years, men have had a very specific role – to provide food for the family/tribe, and to protect family/tribe. This was a system that worked, though not without flaws, but it *worked*.

And it worked for a long time.

It is true that women suffered, but we cannot ignore the fact that men suffered and died too.

Men were the ones who would go out into battle and fight and die for those back home, making every attempt to *prevent* the suffering of women and children. The current feminist movement ignores these sacrifices, but the truth cannot be denied.

There are several lies that are preached *ad nauseum* about the evils of men in our day.

One we are taught is that men are supposed to project an image of being harmless. We are told that this is the *new* ideal man, harmless. I would like to offer the possibility that this is patently false. The ideal man is not harmless. The ideal man is someone who is capable of inflicting great injury, someone who can unleash a violent sadism against those who would harm his family. A capacity for viciousness the likes of which the predator has not only never seen, he has never even imagined. The ideal man will kill those who would harm his family, **but** does not relish the thought of killing. The ideal man *wishes* to harm no one, but will not stand by while someone harms those under his care and protection. The ideal man, in short, is someone who is capable of great violence, but is in total control of when and where this violence will be practiced.

Another lie we are told is that women hate the traditional, tough-as-nails manly man.

This is also false.

Women hate the men who don't understand that no means no, they hate the harassers, and they hate the man-child. But they do not hate the truly traditional man.

There are women who are taught to hate the traditional male and especially when he wants to live his role in the traditional manner. But these women are few. They are loud, and they tend to put into practice most of the masculine traits that they scream are abusive, oppressive, and harmful, but they are still the few.

Yet another lie is that masculinity is *toxic*. One need only look at the decay in society, brought on by this insistence that the structure that worked for thousands of years needs to be cast aside, and it becomes clear what is really and truly toxic.

I would respond to these, and other lies, by offering the simple truth – men serve a very important role in our society. We do not need to *defend* our role, we need only *claim* our birthright.

As men, we are still supposed to provide food and protection for our family. Society does not need to approve of this or claim that it is the right thing for us to do. Screaming, red-faced girls on university campuses claiming to be *triggered* by everything do not *need* to think they need us to protect them from predators, but we can and we should still be *capable* of protecting them nonetheless.

We have a job to do and we must do it.

Providing for the family does not mean that the Wife cannot work, it only means that the man *must* work.

Different people have different stations in life, and some households need two incomes to survive, there is no harm and no shame in this. There is also no shame in the household where the Wife makes more money than the man.

But the man *must* still work. The mental cost of *not*

fulfilling this natural obligation to provide is simply too great to pay.

The man must also be ready, willing, and able to defend his family.

This in no way means that every man must become a black belt martial arts master. It means taking your basic talents, and maximizing your abilities to protect home and Family.

Whatever it takes, learn how defend your family, and train in that method so that, should the need ever arise, you will be prepared and capable of being the man that your family needs.

None of this needs to be done with the hateful attitude of our attackers. The times may be vulgar, we need not be. We can assume our role, as has been done for centuries. No boasting, no demanding, just doing our job, doing what needs to be done without fanfare or attention seeking.

In the pages that follow, we will take a look at some different warrior cultures and their views on being a man. We will also look through the writings of some extraordinarily badass men, and examine their thoughts on the subject.

As we do this, some interesting things will happen.

For a start, we will notice that some very different warrior cultures held the same values as one another, and in many cases these values are held in high regard in our time as well.

How can this be so?

How can an ancient group of "savages" hold the same regard for values that we prize in our modern, socially just, and nontoxic world?

It is simple; some values are universal.

Additionally, our views of these ancient cultures are often clouded by unconscious judgement of their entire society based on how things are done in our time.

Here is but one example. It is no sign of sophistication to claim that modern society does not participate in slavery, and therefore our society is superior, yet this argument is put forward on University campuses all across the U.S. nearly every day. Our society has the benefit of hindsight. We are not worthy enough to criticize the generation that actually *ended* the practice of slavery in the U.S.[1] That group was

---

[1] Slavery is brought up as a major crime against the United States all the time. What is ignored is that slavery was practiced by *all* nations in the past. It was western civilization that ended the practice, and the United States fought a very costly war to end it. And the Founding Fathers, who are so chastised in our day

more dignified and paid a greater cost in blood and treasure to put an end to it than most of our current crop would ever consider paying. And their ending the practice did not contain anything as simple and costless as a hashtag campaign. They fought and were maimed and they died.

This is but one example, but there are plenty of others.

Warrior cultures are often cast aside as brutish because of the rivers of blood which have been shed in wars which we do not have the proper context or education to understand.

But the ethics which were prized by these cultures show quite clearly that they were much more than savage brutes. They were thoughtful, giving, and cared about family. They loved deeply.

It does not take much research to see that they prized family in ways which shame many of the men in our time. Careful consideration was given to the proper way to raise children and help them to fit in to the society into which they had been born.

We would do well to look at our approach to this

---

actually worded things in the founding documents in such a way that the practice of slavery was doomed. They should be given more credit for their part in the abolition of slavery. But this would require actual *thinking*, so I suppose it is too much to ask.

same idea for our own children.

There are those who want to set aside the entire structure of western society. But when we try to cast aside tradition because it is *toxic* to the poorly prepared, we are making a mistake. *All* societies were built upon certain ideas and roles that those in the society were to play. When you try to cast the entire structure aside, you are going to lose all of the supporting framework too!

You can say that the role of Women in traditional societies did not allow women to live up to their full potential. That is fine, and it is also probably spot on in most cases. But when we cast aside the nurturing role of the Mother, then the children are the ones who end up lacking someone to fill that vital role. And then we end up standing around asking stupid questions about why kids are so poorly behaved these days. Women and men both have a traditional role in the raising of children.

The traditional role of the man in raising children is often viewed with scorn. It is taught that, yes, men helped in creating the baby, but then hunted and warred and whored until they died. This is quite false. Men were the providers, they kept the family fed. They were also the protectors, they kept the family safe.

But further still, they were the role model for the

sons and daughters. To the sons, they taught them how to be a man, and what is meant to be a man. A boy cannot learn this from his Mother. To the daughters, they lived as an example of what a man was supposed to be. A girl cannot learn this from her Mother.

Without a doubt, there have been many men who failed to fulfill their role, in both the traditional and modern society. But we must ask, were these men chastised and possibly ostracized from society when they failed in their role? In many societies the answer is yes. In times now gone, men who failed to fulfill their role in society were branded as bad men because of their behavior, and they were treated accordingly. In our time, men are told they are bad because they are men.

Does this make any sense?

As a man, as a Father, and as a person who tries his best to live a life as an example, I say no. Being a male is not an instant guilty verdict. Men today are told that they perpetuate a *rape culture*, and *patriarchy*, and if we deny this, we are declared guilty. Without evidence, we are found guilty, with the accusation being the only proof. Men are told we are evil because we are male.

I have been told that because I am a male, I am a potential rapist. Never mind that I have never, nor will I ever, rape anyone. Simply having the necessary equipment makes you guilty in this supposed utopia that the do-gooders are trying to build.

The method chosen in this book to reject this pseudo-feminist indictment of anything masculine is to examine some warrior cultures and their philosophy of manhood, and to look to the teachings of some ultra badass men and see where their values can be applied in our life today. The obvious rejection of what is presented here will be to lambast the warrior cultures and Badasses outright. Cognitive dissonance being what it is, they will do this regardless of whatever ideas are presented.

I present this book without regard to, or fear of the attacks to come. I am not here to convert modern-wave feminists. Real men want the best for women, and we want all kinds of equal rights for women, and all that was a part of the initial wave of feminism.

Men do not want women to be oppressed at all, we just want to be allowed to be men. Men are not perfect, but neither are women. And many men are starting to reject this *bridge too far* of the latest wave of a philosophy in which all men are evil and have never done anything good for humanity.

Without men being the way that we are and making the sacrifices we have made, just as it has been for women, there might be no humanity left to discuss this.

It takes men *and* women to make this world, this society, and all that goes along with that. It is an act of futility to claim that one gender has all of the answers.

We all have roles to play in society and in life. And before anyone gets all worked up, I want to state a loud **YES**, that there are people who do not fit neatly into the traditional gender roles, they are very few percentagewise, but this does not make them irrelevant. They count as much as anyone else, and they should be able to live their life as they wish, undisturbed, without persecution, penalty, or torment. A rational person can look at things and see that there is no one-size-fits-all answer to every possible combination of circumstances that a few billion different lives may encounter. Claiming otherwise is just fatuous.

As we men look at what is being done with these attacks upon us, we need not be crude, but we can simply say that enough is enough. We can return to what made us men and made us successful in the first place, and we can, in spite of any objections given, look to the best of what made the warrior cultures what they were, and use that as a model or a base from which to restore or reclaim the masculinity of those who came before us. And it will be easier than we have been told. There will just be a few loud voices claiming that we are bad, toxic, and irredeemable.

Ignore them. We have work to do and we do not have time for those who find fault with everything.

What this book is not:

This book in no way whatsoever should be confused with any sort of attack on women. This is not intended to berate, oppress, diminish, abuse or assault women or to ignore all that they contribute to our families, our societies, and our world. Any perception left with the reader that women are to be viewed as *less than* anyone or anything is as misguided and mistaken as humanly possible. If, after actually reading this book, you feel that the intent was to attack women, I suggest a chamomile tea, a good night's sleep, and a reread; because you were clearly not focused on the task of reading the first time around.

This book is in no way shape or form an attack on gay people. Gay men are not less of a man, they are just men, end of discussion. This book is written in defense of all men. Period. A person's sexual preferences are their own, and are not up for debate. Men are men.

A man can let people live their own life.

Some people want to take views to extreme points where no one ever intended, and these people cannot be accounted for. But the real meaning of tolerance is that you let people live their own lives, while you live yours.

One cannot claim to be tolerant without allowing people to be left to their own fate. This includes people doing things you might disagree with personally. For the things you disagree with, do not do them. If another person chooses to do them, you need to remind yourself that you only live your own life, and they only live theirs. We all make our decisions based on the best that we know to do, and it is not our place to dictate terms to others, we have our own life to live.

If you still think that this book is about attacking instead of defending, then I cannot help you.

1 Lakota Sioux

Category: Warrior Culture
Origin: North America

The Lakota Sioux were warriors of high regard. Their homeland was in the American states of North and South Dakota. In our day, there are only around 70,000 Lakota Sioux, and as with many other tribes, the numbers of the tribe who still speak the ancestral language is dwindling, and the tribe today is but a shadow of their glorious past.

But in their day...

The Sioux are, rightfully, a proud people. Their tribe was huge and they controlled a large portion of the land in North America, spanning from the Great Lakes to the Rocky Mountains. They were feared by many other tribes throughout their history.

The Sioux were known to be great warriors. Their reputation struck fear into the hearts of many, but within their tribe, Family was central to everything.

The Sioux term for children was *Wakanisha* (sacred).

While the men were allowed to take more than one Wife, infidelity was severely punished.

As with all traditional cultures, men were expected to provide for, and defend the family. Women were respected and ruled over the domestic lives of the family, but the men were men; expected to hunt for food and defend the tribe and family.

Fighting with other tribes, war, was an important time for a Sioux man. A man had the opportunity to gain honor and prestige for their family through acts of bravery in battle.

As American settlers began to occupy the Sioux lands, and several treaties with the American government were made and routinely broken, the Sioux retaliated against the much more powerful and better equipped Americans. The result was three major Indian wars.

In 1854 at Fort Laramie in Wyoming, there was a battle in which 19 U.S. soldiers were killed. In response, the U.S. troops killed 100 Sioux in Nebraska. Chief Red Cloud fought a war that ended in 1867, and in the treaty that ended the war, the Sioux were granted the Black Hills *in perpetuity*.

This was not to be, however, as gold was discovered in the Black Hills, and American fortune hunters simply went into the hills in search of treasure without government permission or regard for treaties. It was the treasure hunters who brought about further wars, the most famous of which ended with the death of 300 U.S. troops and took the life of the renowned General George Custer at Little Big Horn.

This massacre of the U.S. troops resulted in the overkill of 370 men, women, and children at Wounded Knee. The Sioux were utterly defeated at this point, with only a few holdouts continuing to fight from this point forward.

The mighty Sioux were defeated. To our great benefit, they adapted and were able to pass on their wisdom to us.

Within the reservation lands, the Tribe is its own

Nation today, and as such has its own laws and government. Many try to preserve their heritage by passing on to the next generation training in the traditional morals and values.

There are listed what are called the 12 Lakota Virtues. In this chapter we will explore these virtues and try to discover the meaning they might have for our modern life.

Unsiiciyap (Humility).

In times much harsher than our own, every member of the tribe served the tribe. Feelings of pride are part of human nature, but one must not forget that the tribe made survival possible.

The person who has to take credit for everything is annoying to us. In times past, this person was divisive in a situation where unity might mean the difference between life and death. Unity was paramount.

In the ancient past, the first humans discovered that we could accomplish more, survive longer, and eat better, through the seemingly simple act of working together, than we ever could working alone. Over time, this caused a value to be placed on humility.

The value is still carried by most of us today. It should be put into practice by men everywhere.

You can begin to put it into practice be remembering to value the thoughts and opinions of others. Place some attention and value in the simple act of listening and always keep in mind that not everything is about you.

Humility also prevents people from prejudging most of your actions. The boastful braggart is instantly mistrusted when they are showing concern. There are always people who will help someone just to say they were the one who did it.

Wowaci ntanka (Perseverance).

Part of being a good member of the tribe, one who produces and, much more than providing for themselves, actually provides enough to help support the tribe as a whole, is found in perseverance.

When times were tough, sometimes food was scarce.

In our day, we can walk into a store and purchase freshly ground meat and just picked produce. Many of our ancestors would be amazed at the ease at which we can get food, and they would be baffled at our ability to be depressed while having things so good.

For the Sioux, if the days hunt didn't work out well, the quitter might be having a splash in a pity-puddle. This does no good for the individual, but it is also a problem for the tribe. One must fulfill their role for the good of the tribe. Perseverance is the virtue which brings the individual to push hard and keep trying when they might otherwise want to quit.

For the modern man, the tribe is replaced with family. We do our part by providing food, shelter, and protection. The first two are done through our work. Perseverance is *vital* to work ethic, which is what will set us apart in the workplace. This is but one example, but I am sure you can find others.

Wawoohhola (Respect).

Each person has a role to fulfill. Each person provides a crucial service. Each person *matters*.

In our time, people are quick to judge certain people as being beneath them, and thus deserving little to no respect. But take a moment to consider the role being fulfilled by the trash collector. While you disrespect his job, he is providing a service that you truly need!

You might be irritated at the Semi on the highway, but you really do want those goods delivered to your local grocer.

You may think of the plumber or the AC repairman as being far beneath your station in life, but when you need their services, you really want them there, and you want your problem solved *now*.

These people are providing for their family just as you do for yours. It does not diminish you to respect their humanity.

In fact, disrespecting their humanity diminishes *your* worth. Showing respect to others does harms no one. Respect is an essential in so many aspects of life. Being a respectful person will never offend anyone, even in our ultra-sensitive modern society. So, show some respect! If you want people to respect you, then being respectful is required.

Wayyuonihan (Honor).

Many people struggle to understand the concept of honor. It really isn't that complicated. Respect is a way of recognizing the worth of every other person. Honor is what you do to be worthy of having them respect *your* worth.

If you are going to view anything as being beneath you, it should be anything that makes you unworthy of respect.

This is not unrelated to the Asian concept of *Face*. When you understand the concept of face, then it makes more sense. This is working toward doing nothing which gives people a reason to *not* respect you. It is making sure that people know you are a man of integrity.

Dishonesty, greed, selfishness. These are things that make you a person of less value to others (your tribe).

People want to be recognized and respected, but often they take shortcuts that make them unworthy of such praise. Don't be that guy. Instead, be the guy who is dependable, hard-working, loves his family, and isn't afraid to do the difficult work.

Being a person of honor is really about doing the right thing. It isn't always easy to do the right thing, and is usually isn't convenient, but right is right.

Cantognake (Love).

People tend to get really confused about love. They think that love might be lust, or a sexual feeling, or sweet words. Others think it is a powerful emotion.

They are all wrong.

Love is a behavior.

Love is the *action* of caring for others. Love is setting aside your own wants and desires for the good of another person. It is putting their needs above your own.

For many years, I thought of love as an emotion. I was wrong.

Love as a behavior is a powerful understanding. It allows you to see that simply *thinking* that you love someone is not enough, you must *show* them by your actions every day and every chance you get.

Saying you love someone is simply not enough. Children understand this better than adults do in our time. Love take action.

If you are to be a man who truly loves someone, you will need to be a man of action. You will need to be a man who does what he says. If a man says he loves someone, but treats them like garbage, then he is showing that he is a liar. Live our love as an action and not just another word you use.

Icicup (Sacrifice).

Again we find a running theme. Sacrifice involves placing the needs of others above your own personal wants. You give up something for the good of others. Sacrifice is a manifestation of love. In truth, sacrifice is inseparable from love if one understands love as a behavior.

In looking at the world of the Lakota in the past,

there would be times when you might not eat your fill in order to ensure that everyone in the tribe ate.

Most of us do not have to make such choices, and that is why we do not understand this simple point.

Every good parent understands sacrifice. There is not a parent in the world that couldn't have been better off financially by simply not having children. It is *known* by parents, but never *dwelled* upon.

Parents sacrifice daily for the benefit of their children, and most parents do so without complaint or second thought.

Fathers sacrifice time at home in order to provide for the Family. Mothers sacrifice other aspects of personal fulfillment in order to nurture and love the child.

Sacrifice in the outward manifestation of love for the tribe, doing without so that others can be better off.

Wowicake (Truth).

There are times when we are all tempted to lie in order to escape the consequences of our actions. Most of us were experts at this behavior when we were children, and for the most part the act has been outgrown.

Some people are unable or unwilling to outgrow the habit, and are known forevermore as liars.

Telling lies limits you more than it frees you. Your circle of friends will be ever dwindling as people wise up to what kind of person you are. Lies can also be dangerous, to ourselves and to others.

The truth is not always easy. Sometimes the truth might lessen our personal status if it is known. But there are times when we must pay the piper and own up. Some matters are of great importance to others, and they must know the truth in order to make the proper choices. If we withhold the truth in those circumstances, we are doing something much worse than avoiding our own consequences – we are setting up others to take a fall that we might have prevented. Remember that they are basing their decisions on what they believe to be the truth that they are hearing from us.

Truthfulness isn't always easy, but it is usually the right thing to do.

Waunsilapi (Compassion).

Within the tribe, compassion will achieve greater unity. Unity brings people to a point where they work together better than they can otherwise.

It is common to tell people that you *feel their pain,*

but in truth, you can't. You can only feel your own pain, but you *can* care. And that is what compassion is; the ability to feel concern for the suffering or misfortunes of others.

It shouldn't be difficult to show authentic compassion. It starts with a simple understanding.

Think of the biggest problem in your life right now. To you it might even feel like the biggest problem in the entire world, but to others it is just your issue. They have their own problems to worry about. Understanding that their problem is as real and as grave to them as your problem is to you will allow you to feel compassion.

When I was a kid this was referred to as *putting yourself in their shoes*. And it is something that simply isn't done much anymore.

People in our time Prefer to pass judgement. If you can take a moment to see things form the other person's perspective, your behavior will change a lot, and you can become that better person that we all want to be.

Woohitike (Bravery).

Within the warrior cultures, bravery is prized universally. This is not the reckless, berserker mentality or the lone wolf with a death wish. Quite the contrary, this is about ensuring that everyone goes home.

The brave are not without fear. Fear is a human emotion that happens to all of us. But the brave are those who are able to remain clear-headed and do what needs to be done, no matter what is going on around them.

Bravery is also a choice. One must be willing to make the tough decisions and walk toward danger in order to be brave.

Every hero in history had a choice, they could have walked away from the danger and the risk to life and limb in the hope that *someone else will do it*.

The brave *knew* they had the option to back out, but they didn't.

Why?

It isn't because of a lack of fear. It isn't because of a mental disorder. It isn't because they couldn't see the other options. And it most certainly wasn't because of "toxic masculinity".

The bravest knew and saw everything in front of them, and simply did what had to be done. Not because there was no one else to do it. They did it so that no one else would *have* to do it.

Being brave does not ensure personal victory or glory. Many brave people lost their lives on the field of battle all over the planet, and rivers have run red with the blood of heroes.

But the brave are also those who give an edge to those around them. They can be counted on to make the tough decisions and press forward when others might still be frozen in the rotten ground of indecision.

Cantewasake (Fortitude).

Fortitude is taking a step beyond courage and bravery. Fortitude has to do with being courageous while suffering pain or hardship.

This is an important aspect of warrior culture that is often overlooked.

It is a good thing to be brave. It is quite another to be brave after taking damage. This is assuredly a rarer trait. When a person who has been shot allows the Hollywood mental image to take over, they will fall down and not try to get back up. And they *will* die. The classic movie line, "Go on without me!" comes to mind.

A warrior cannot afford to lay down after being wounded. He *must* get back up and get back into the fight. He has too many people counting on him. This is what drives him, compels him to return to the fight.

In our time, it is easy to find examples of fortitude. Many men who find themselves fired from job they held for a decade or two will simply spend the rest of their days feeling defeated. But there are those who bounce back. They regroup, and they fight back.

Often one is tempted to ask if a man was defeated, or if he surrendered. When you have people counting on you, then there are times you have to man up, recognized that you took a hit, and get back into the fight.

We were designed for this. It is a lot easier if you are committed to the fight, but simply feeling responsible for others can be enough to keep a man focused on the real task at hand, and let him avoid the pity-puddle of self-sorrow.

Canteyuke (Generosity).

Generosity cannot be compelled. It cannot be coerced. Generosity starts as compassion. It starts with caring.

In the warrior cultures one finds a running theme of these hardened killers who actually love deeply, much more so than our modern deadbeats who abandon a woman as soon as she is pregnant.

The warriors of old, the men who were our forefathers, they loved deeply.

In loving deeply, one is able to want to ease the suffering of those we care about. We will even try to prevent them from suffering at all if we can do so. In this line of thought, we will give what we have to them.

All that we have, even up to and including our very lives, will be given without a second thought.

Throughout history, the lives of men were what was expendable. We never backed down from this responsibility until very recently. Giving up our lives for the sake of the tribe, the village, the family, was part and parcel of being a man.

There is no greater generosity. Do not be reckless, but be prepared to pay any price to protect those you love and who are under your care.

Woksape (Wisdom).

Should he be lucky enough to live a long and full life, a man is imbued with wisdom. Not a smarty-pants type of know-it-all BS, but actual wisdom.

Real wisdom is the aggregate of experience, knowledge, common sense, insight and understanding. This is why the young are seldom considered wise.

In traditional cultures, the old were venerated because they had life experiences that would allow them to make better decisions that the young could.

And the young went to them for answers.

In warrior cultures, the old warriors had to be venerated because many warriors simply didn't survive to reach old age, and their wisdom went to the grave with them. Those who did survive must have seemed more God than man. This is who we speak of when we are talking about heroes.

Wisdom is underappreciated in our time. People in our time have a soundbite addiction and a factual deficit. Many people prize a snarky comeback over actual wisdom. This is worse than sad.

One step in reclaiming masculinity is in refusing to accept the labels given to men by those too ignorant to appreciate the wisdom which allowed our entire species to survive as long as it has.

Start by renewing your study of those wise men of old who helped their people survive and thrive.

Notes: The lifestyle of the Lakota Sioux is just about as far removed from our modern lifestyle as anything we are likely to find.

Having said that, we can see from these twelve virtues that they were as noble as any group of humans we can name. There is hardly a person on this planet who would disagree with holding *any* of these virtues in high regard.

Modern people seem to view the American Indians as being either brutish savages, or harmless people who were destroyed be evil white people.

Both thoughts are baseless and ignorant. While there were some tribes who were more peaceful than others, the simple fact remains that theirs was a different age. We have little to compare that age to in our own time, except perhaps street gang culture[2]. Each tribe had territory, and defended it fiercely. To those outside of the tribe, other tribes were likely seen as evil and savage, but inside of the tribe, the warriors were heroes.

We tend to overlook this and remain blind to it in our own time.

But if we allow ourselves to see that the American Indians were what they were, peaceful at times, and viciously war-like at other times, we can see the truth better, and see that these values are a powerful statement.

For a people who were as skilled at war as the Lakota Sioux were to prize such values as

---

[2] This is not intended as an insult to the Native American Indian, for whom I have much respect, and with whom I share blood. It is nothing more than an analogy.

humility, perseverance, respect, honor, love, sacrifice, truth, compassion, bravery, fortitude, generosity, and wisdom shows that, although living in a savage world, they were a people who were noble and strong.

We can learn from them. We can learn about being strong and upright in a world that is cruel and rudderless.

Make no mistake, our world has a façade of moral superiority to any culture which came before us, but it is a thin veneer. The Lakota Sioux were much more in touch with their humanity than many people in our modern age, and we could do a lot worse than to learn from them about how to be a good man.

2 The Shaolin Temple

Category: Religious doctrine, influenced by retired
warriors entering temple life
Origin: China

It is believed by many that all martial arts trace their beginnings to the Shaolin Temple in Hunan Province of China.

To believe this, there are a certain set of mental gymnastics that must be done, starting with the simple fact that the different empires which eventually united to form what we know as China all had standing armies long before the Shaolin temple was ever built. These armies trained their soldiers, and this is true martial art[3].

In truth, the Shaolin temple did not start off as a training ground for warrior monks. It was just another temple at the foot of just another mountain.

Over time, Military Generals ended up retiring to the temple, for reasons lost to the proverbial mists of time. These retired military men would have come to the temple well versed in military strategy, weapon use, and hand-to-hand fighting skills. No doubt, some of them would have had a hand in training the younger monks. It is most likely that the martial arts of Shaolin come from these beginnings, far more likely than the traditional Bodhidharma story.

Such skills would have been handy in an age where there were bandits along all of the roads from city to city and security was expensive, so having security provided in house would make sense.

There is little doubt among scholars that martial

---

[3] The word "martial" in martial arts has its root in Mars, the Roman God of war. Military training is *real* martial art.

arts existed in China at least as far back as 2500 BCE. The story of Bodhidharma leaving India and arriving at Shaolin in 428 A.D. to create Shaolin Kung fu and thus, all martial arts, is well known and well worn, but it is unlikely at best.

What is known to be true is that there was travel and trade between India and China. The roads were dangerous, with threats from both human and animal attacks, and as such, measures would have been taken to ensure personal safety when traveling these roads.

It was during this time that the monks from the Shaolin temple began to train with the retired generals living with them. They learned to fight, and this physical exercise was viewed mostly as another method of meditation, a moving meditation.

Defensive fighting skills were needed, but they must be squared away with the temple's religious doctrine[4].

---

[4] As might be expected, the monks had a very strict life with many rules which must be obeyed. In Buddhism, there is a strict rule against killing, and a high value placed on a peaceful life. Any martial arts training which was aggressive and deadly would have been off-limits except in the direst circumstances.

This need was met by the idea of *Wu De* (Martial Morality).

Wu De codified the ideas of self-defense in such a way that the devotees of Shaolin orthodoxy were able to harden their bodies and remain tender-hearted enough to care about their follow human beings and their sufferings.

Highest among the ideals of Wu De are respect, humility, trust, virtue, and honor.

Zun Jing; 尊敬 *(Respect).*

Tied closely to the eastern concept of Face, respect in this sense is about treating others in such a way that they are never diminished by your words or actions.

This, in turn, prevents feelings of ill will toward you.

This is in no way to be seen as an act of cowardice, acting in fear of conflict. On the contrary, this is done to build up another person in front of those who hold him in esteem.

Does it diminish you to show respect to another person, recognizing the value of the role they play in their own sphere of influence?

Absolutely not!

In fact, through the act of building others up, *you* are built up in the eyes of others. In this way, the servant and the served are one and the same.

Qian Xu; 谦逊 (Humility).

Humility in the trait that caused the first Europeans visiting to write that the Chinese are "possessed of an inhuman self-control."

Self-control leads to a drop in impulsive behavior, and as we all know, impulsive behavior leads to regret.

Humility also allows us to never reach that point where we feel that we know everything we need to know. With humility we will continue to study and to train with the idea of becoming better.

Within the martial arts, the best are those who train to become better, not to attain a high rank or to be addressed by this or that title. It is about the training of the skill.

The best martial artists understand that the journey *is* the goal.

It should be a part of the worldview of every man to view himself as a student. There is always more to learn, no matter how much you think you know. If there are three people walking toward you, it is likely that at least one of them could teach you something, and probable that all three could do so.

The beginner's mind will not only keep you humble, it will keep you interested.

Xin Yong: 信用 (Trust).

Trust is built over a period of time. It can be lost in a very short period of time, perhaps even in an instant.

Because trust must be built over time, there are many who are unwilling to put in the effort over time that is required.

But for people to see that as a good choice, forgoing the trust of others, there must be some sort of a payoff for them.

What would that payoff be?

For a start, being trustworthy is a pretty big responsibility. It requires you to follow through on your words with action.

Making big promises is something politicians do very well, but they are quite poor at fulfilling those promises.

Not having any responsibility, being free to say whatever you want, but being unwilling or unable to back up your word must be liberating in some sense, because there are a lot of people who simply don't care to be trustworthy.

The downside to that, of course, is that you miss out on the deeper and much more rewarding relationships with people.

When they trust you, there is a much better payoff in that you get to deepen that trust.

Because trust is a two-way street, it is important to ask, how trusting are *you* of other people?

Placing your trust in people opens up the possibility of disappointment.

Scratch that, people *will* disappoint you.

Sometimes they will disappoint you over and over if you keep them in your life long enough.

The proverbial tough-guy would say that people are not worth trusting. But sometimes you have to give a person a *chance to fail* before they will ever be able to prove themselves.

There are times when, given the chance, people will prove out.

Others will take advantage of you.

Which way is the right way?

The truth is that each person is different, a unique

case. And if you also consider that each person is fundamentally changed by each challenge they face in life, you will start to see that there is not always an easy way to see if a person worth the risk of trusting them.

Sometimes you will be right, and other times you will be wrong, but these are choices that you must make for yourself.

Be a person who is worthy of the trust of others. Be slow to promise, but quick to perform. Follow through on your word, mean what you say. Be honest with others. In this you will be worthy of trust.

Trust other people. Give them a chance whenever possible or reasonable. You don't want to just be another person who drops the line on a person when what they really needed was a chance. But don't be a doormat.

Yes, all of this can be confusing. This is because real world problems don't have easy answers.

Rong Yu; 榮譽 (Honor).

Honor is a difficult concept for many people to understand. Honor is tied to being truthful, trustworthy, and yet there is a sense that it is something more.

It is really about living a life of meaning.

How many people do you know, or perhaps you are one of these people, people who live day to day with no plan, no goals, and no spark.

The rudderless existence makes the game not worth the candle.

In order to live a life of meaning, you have to have a goal and you have to allow nothing to cause you to deviate from the goal. You have to live by a code, and you have to stick to your code of conduct, ~~even~~ especially when it is not easy to do so.

Being a person of honor comes with a cost.

You will lose friends that you do not want to lose, and sometimes you will be the one to send them out of your life. You will miss out on many things that might distract you or take you off of your path.

But if the path is honorable, and if the goal is worth your time and effort, then you need to do what must be done.

There is no real success that comes without sacrifice.

A man must stand through the storms and do what is right.

Always.

De; 德 (Virtue).

In American culture, most people have a bad image of virtue. Most people who hear the word virtue think of moral busybodies, religious zealots who want to lord it over the private lives of others.

In a classic case of turnaround, half of the population in America adopted politics as their religion, and proceeded to become political busybodies trying to lord over the private thoughts and public words of everyone in the country. This is painfully sad to watch.

But in the sense as used by the Chinese, virtue is to be taken more as a natural innate quality than a sense of moral superiority.

Think of when we speak of the healing virtues of a certain plant. The virtue referenced by the Chinese word *de* is like this, but applied to humans.

Humans all share certain qualities. Everyone wants to do what they see as good. The precise definition of good varies greatly, but nearly all people are seeking the good.

Nearly all people are also seeking to avoid their own suffering. Most will push suffering onto others if it mean that they, themselves, will not have to suffer.

If this is recognized and admitted, then we can start from a point of honesty with ourselves.

We must recognize that no one is perfect. We are all both loving and selfish, courageous and cowards, just and unjust. Knowing this, we are able to be less judgmental toward others.

This sense of virtue has nothing to do with being better than others, and everything to do with being the best *we* can be.

When we focus on doing what we are supposed to do, and being the best that we can be, we have less time to criticize others. We get more done through the simple act of paying attention to what we are doing.

Place your focus on being your absolute best. Give 100% of what you have toward fulfilling your obligations every day, even if your 100% on that day is less than your normal 100% - give all that you have toward being your best. In this, you will find *de*.

Notes: From the Shaolin Temple we learn that a man can be tough, warrior tough, and yet seek spiritual fulfillment. This does not lessen the man. Quite the contrary, it expands the mind and improves his life in many ways.

Whether or not one believes in any religion, or

none at all, there is still a lot to be learned that will improve our relationships with our loved ones though the study of things spiritual or psychological. Many religions contain extensive teachings in areas of interpersonal relationships and societal well-being, just as psychology books contain many unexplained phenomena involving poorly understood aspects of the mind.

What matters is study and self-improvement.

Within the martial arts, there is typically a high regard for the heritage from Shaolin. For the modern man, the idea of combining the badass with the deeply spiritual is, if nothing else, very refreshing. In our day we seem to be forced to make a choice between being a tough person capable of visiting great violence upon those who would do us harm, and being a spiritual person who is concerned with living a life free of conflict. With the approach of Shaolin, we see a path toward being fully immersed in the study of things spiritual, while honing the body into a weapon of great power, power which will be devastatingly used if the need ever arises.

Taken at a different angle we can say that a man can be a warrior without always looking for a war to fight. Train the body to be able to survive any conflict, but also train the mind to be able to discern *when and if* things require violence.

3 Sparta

Category: Warrior Culture
Origin: Greece

The warriors of Sparta are both legend and fact.

They were as deadly an army as has ever existed. They have earned a place of awe and respect from every man who has ever prepared for battle. While all stories of the great warriors of Sparta are not necessarily true, with the Spartans, there isn't really a need to make up fake stories. They were amazing in truth.

Sparta was a part of Greece. They were independent people whose citizens trained in what can only be accurately described as the archetype warrior society. Without a doubt, they were the most feared military force of their time.

It was noted by many that one Spartan was worth several men from any other state.

Lycurgus is credited with creating the military focus of the Spartan male's life.

The life of the Spartan male as a soldier began as an infant when he was inspected. If he was found to have weakness or deformity, he was left on Mount Taygetus to die of exposure.

Those not left to die entered into military training at the age of seven. This training consisted mainly of sports and war tactics. Contrary to popular imagery, there was also training in non-military arts (music, poetry, and politics).

The Spartan man lived in such a way that actual war was a welcome interruption from the constant training for war. It has been noted by several historians that the training of the Spartan warrior was so strict that *actual* war was a relief.

If one has doubts as to the bravery of the Spartan warriors, one need only look closer. There is a retelling of an Athenian who questioned why the

Spartan sword was so short, and the Spartan replied that the sword was long enough to reach the heart. There was no desire to fight at a distance, if you were close enough, there was room enough. There is another story of a Spartan boy who complained that his sword was too short, and his mother told him to step closer to his enemy.

In the battle of Thermopylae, Spartan King Leonidas and his famous 300 man army held off an advance by the Persian King Xerces, whose army numbered about 100, 000 – 150,000. The Spartans fought to the death knowing that they had no chance at victory.

Fighting at such a disadvantage might be considered insane by some, but it was simply what the men of Sparta did.

Although their lifestyle is not something that could ever be imitated in our time, their ideals and views can still give the modern man an insight into a very strong masculinity that is sorely lacking in much of modern society.

The Spartan Creed

I would not say anything for a man nor take account of him for any speed of his feet or wrestling skill he might have, not if he had the size of a Cyclops and strength to go with it, not if he could outrun Bóreas, the North

Wind of Thrace, not if he were more handsome and gracefully formed than Tithónos, or had more riches than Midas had, or Kínyras too, not if he were more of a king than Tantalid Pelops, or had the power of speech and persuasion Adrastos had, not if he had all splendors except for a fighting spirit.

For no man ever proves himself a good man in war unless he can endure to face the blood and the slaughter, go close against the enemy and fight with his hands. Here is courage, mankind's finest possession, here is the noblest prize that a young man can endeavor to win, and it is a good thing his city and all the people share with him when a man plants his feet and stands in the foremost spears relentlessly, all thought of foul flight completely forgotten, and has well trained his heart to be steadfast and to endure, and with words encourages the man who is stationed beside him.

Here is a man who proves himself to be valiant in war. With a sudden rush he turns to fight the rugged battalions of the enemy, and sustains the beating waves of assault. And he who so falls among the champions and loses his sweet life, so blessing with honor his city, his father, and all his people, with wounds in his chest, where the spear that he was facing has transfixed that massive guard of his shield, and gone through his breastplate as well, why, such a man is lamented alike by the young and the elders, and all his city goes into mourning and grieves for his loss. His tomb is pointed to with pride, and so are his children, and his children's children, and afterward all the race that is his. His

shining glory is never forgotten, his name is remembered, and he becomes an immortal, though he lies under the ground, when one who was a brave man has been killed by the furious War God standing his ground and fighting hard for his children and land. But if he escapes the doom of death, the destroyer of bodies, and wins his battle, and bright renown for the work of his spear, all men give place to him alike, the youth and the elders, and much joy comes his way before he goes down to the dead. Aging, he has reputation among his citizens. No one tries to interfere with his honors or all he deserves; all men withdraw before his presence, and yield their seats to him, the youth, and the men his age, and even those older than he. Thus a man should endeavor to reach this high place of courage with all his heart, and, so trying, never be backward in war. –
Tyrtaeus

The Spartan culture held certain traits in the highest regard, and many of these traits *are* directly applicable to modern men who are searching for the best of what a man is supposed to put into practice.

Equals.

In Sparta, men referred to one another as equals. This is significant in that many quarrels are avoided when one does not feel superior to another, or feel owed certain praise due to being superior themselves. When men view one another as equals, then it becomes much easier to work together.

It is quite possible in our time to put this into practice. In terms of the martial arts, one can find many examples of instructors who demand to be called "master", or "grandmaster", and even "master of masters". But these people are usually the subject of derision behind their backs.

If you are not respected when your back is turned, you are not truly respected at all.

Treating others as if they are your equal allows for finding common ground, and even friendship.

Consider how you treat others, especially those to whom you feel that you owe nothing. Do you even speak to the office janitorial staff? You should! If they were not doing their job, you would surely suffer. Show some appreciation. Every person has a role to play and is important in that role.

Service.

All occupations in Sparta were outlawed, with the exception of military service. Until the age of sixty, a man was a soldier. All other occupations were unbecoming a man.

Obviously, in our time not every man is going to be a soldier in the military. But this does not mean that a man cannot serve. Men have a primary role that they must play if they are to feel that primal and ancient fulfillment.

We are, first and foremost, protectors. It is the men who have always been the traditional protectors of the tribe, village, and family. It is our birthright and our duty.

As such, every man should learn to fight, use weapons and firearms, and be prepared mentally and physically to perform the task of protecting home and hearth. This is a service every man can take up, if only they will. If we view it as something *owed by us* to our community, then we will do what must be done out of a sense of obligation.

Get the training necessary to claim your position as a protector.

Community of Men.

The Spartans ate together. Every meal was in a "common mess". This was done with the intent that the men would bond as a team, a military unit that would fight to save the life of their brothers. In our time, men hanging out with men is discouraged. Men being men is viewed with suspicion and often ridicule.

Ignore this and do what needs to be done.

There is something primal in going hunting with men. It is in our DNA. Hunting is an easy example to use because in addition to protecting the home, men were traditionally charged with hunting for food. Men have always done this in groups to ensure greater success. When men get together with buddies today to go hunting, or when a Father teaches his son to hunt, there is a connection to the past that men who do not partake will never know.

Of course, there is a deeper meaning behind the community of men. When men are friends and consider one another to be brothers, and this is what allowed the Spartans at Thermopylae to fight, not for self, but for their brother in arms standing next to them. They were not fighting for glory or honor or even self. They fought out of love for a brother. This is part of what allowed the three-hundred to hold off an army of 150,000 as long as they did.

Selfishness could never accomplish such a feat.

Warriors who were fighting to save the life of the warrior standing next to them did the impossible.

To the man who has never had a brother, blood relative or otherwise, it might be difficult to grasp. When you have that bond with someone, you can bear any burden except failing your brothers.

Selflessness.

There is a reason that selflessness has been traditionally respected, it is a virtue that serves others and makes them feel valued. It is also an act that few people can demonstrate.

Because men have been traditionally called upon to defend the home even if it costs us our lives, it is supposed to be an innate skill that we have. In our time, the constant beating down of any and all things masculine has led to the eminent disaster of the whiny, selfish man-child.

In a classic example of throwing the baby out with the bathwater, our modern world has thrown selflessness out with all of the other masculine traits which were deemed *toxic*.

Selflessness is often necessary. If a man is to sacrifice time at home in order to earn and provide, then this has to be a good trait. If it is classified as a toxic trait, then there will be an increase of broken homes and fatherless children, because sitting in your parent's basement playing video games is a lot easier and less stressful than being a father.

A man must be willing and able to sacrifice his personal wants for the good of the family.

Notes: In our time, men are berated for being men

and doing what men do. It does us good to be reminded that men were *needed* to be men for thousands of years before this modern nonsense started, and *men* will be needed again.

The men of Sparta were more like us than we might imagine. It would be a mistake to say that they are so far removed from modern men that we cannot learn from them.

Their understanding and cherishing brotherhood would be one fact among many that we should be able to see at a glance that we need to have in our life. Any man can understand this ideal. Men need male friends, and we thrive when we have that feeling of brotherhood.

Placing at the top of our list of priorities the responsibility to protect those we love is to share an instant connection to the men of Sparta. This is what men are born for and our highest purpose in life.

To set aside time for the training of mind and body to be sure we are prepared to protect should the need arise is an act of manhood so basic it seems to be needless to say, and it would be needless to say it if not for the constant attack on men being men. We are to provide food and protection to our family/tribe/village, and any philosophy which states otherwise is flawed. If you can legally be armed, be armed! If not, make your body a weapon and always ready to act.

And should the time ever come that you need to act in defense of your family, fight like the Spartan, willing to do anything, even if it means sacrificing your own life. This does not mean throwing your life away recklessly. This means using the best of your training, knowledge and skills to get the job done, without pausing to consider personal cost.

4 Miyamoto Musashi

Category: General Badass
Origin: Japan

Miyamoto Musashi is often referred to as the *Sword Saint* of Japan. His exploits have spawned hundreds of movies, thousands of stories, and his legend reaches far beyond Japan.

We are told that Musashi left home at the age of 15, leaving behind all of his possessions. He traveled and fought in duels. He fought in a series of duels against one famous school of swordsmanship, the Yoshioka School, defeating leader after leader. This so angered the school that they set up an ambush in order to kill Musashi. He found out about the ambush and attacked the saboteurs by surprise. During this fight Musashi ended up fighting with two swords drawn, which led to his creation of his famous two sword style.

There are stories that Musashi fought in more than sixty duels, and he was never defeated.

In one such duel, Musashi arrived late (as he was known to do), and instead of a sword, he used a bokken (wooden practice sword), which he is said to have carved from a boat oar. Was this from insanity or stratagem, or confidence? We cannot know.

He died in 1645, at the age of 62. He died on one knee, sword in his belt. He had finished writing his final book, the Dokkodo, the Way of Walking Alone, shortly before his death.

He died far beyond the general life expectancy of a warrior in his time. In this chapter, we will look at the Dokkodo and how it may be applied to our lives today in the search to reclaim masculinity.

Musashi's Dokkodo

1. Accept everything just the way it is.

At face value, this is quite sound. One may worry over every little detail of everything possible, or one may opt to accept what is, for our purposes here we can look at this as accepting what cannot be changed.

Sometimes things will go your way, and at other times they will not. What happens to you in life is largely beyond your control. However, your *reaction* to what happens *is* under your control, and you should do the best you can. Leave the whining and crying to the weak. Face things the way they are and be strive to succeed in spite of the challenges.

Wishing that the world were different is easy, but it is also childish. It is important to be able to see and accept that things are the way they are.

There are things that are under your control, things you can change if you decide to change them.

But there are also things that are not under your control. These are the things that you must accept, because all else is going to leave you shooting bullets at the sun. You will be making a grand display over your futile actions, and in the end absolutely nothing will be changed. Opt for being productive.

2. Do not seek pleasure for its own sake.

A man must endure hardships. There are many people who throw their entire life away over trivialities that become addictions. Pleasure for the sake of pleasure is the road to alcoholism, drug addiction, and many worse outcomes.

We all want to seek out pleasure. We all wish to avoid pain and suffering, but sometimes it is not possible; in life we *will* get hurt and we *will* suffer. As men we are to gather ourselves together and press on, regardless of our personal trials.

Don't let these things ruin your life. Keep your eyes focused on your goals and responsibilities. In the end, you will look back on a better life.

Rather than a life spent in pursuit of that floating/falling feeling of drunkenness, seek the rewarding feeling of seeing your children, properly raised, finding their place in life and society. Instead of seeking a number goal in terms of sexual relationships, choose the much more rewarding option of a lifetime partner, and seek to deepen that relationship.

There are many other ways to have a life full of meaning, and sensory pleasure is very fleeting and does nothing to broaden the spirit. We can, and we should all seek, to do better than that.

3. Do not depend on a partial feeling.

A man has to be sure of certain things before taking action. Going through life on a wing and a prayer might sound awesome, but it is no real way to live.

Having goals means that you are not drifting through life. It allows you to keep your focus and make better, more informed decisions.

Of course, there are times when you must make a decision with little information and almost no time for well-reasoned thought. But this is not, or at least should not, be a regular part of your daily life.

Regarding the bigger decisions, think things through and move ahead with full confidence.

And in this instance, confidence is the essential.

Confidence in no way ensures success or even correct decision-making. However, in any state of less than full confidence, you are basically just guessing. In important matters, whenever possible, do not rely on guesswork. Gather all of the essential information you can, bring in educated opinions if possible, and consider all options. In this way you can make a decision of confidence rather than guessing.

Being the best you can be rarely happens by chance, it really takes time, effort, patience, and thought.

4. *Think lightly of yourself, and deeply of the world.*

This is advice that the people of our time should really take to heart. We live in an age where people are seeking internet fame by any means necessary. They do things that are over-the-top disrespectful, blatantly deranged, and insanely dangerous, all in an effort to get people to notice them.

That's not good.

Conceited and self-absorbed people are truly annoying. Never allow yourself to become someone that you would not want around.

When you think too highly of yourself, you will stop listening to others. When you stop listening to others, you will miss out on a lot of really good advice and shared experiences.

Allow yourself to think of others. Listen when they need an ear, be there for those who are depending on you. This does not lessen your masculinity, it enhances it. Don't kiss ass, but be good to your friends. Being a man does not mean that you have to be a cruel hardass to everyone you meet. You will make mistakes, but you will learn from them.

And remember, we are to learn from our own mistakes as well as the mistakes of others, because we will not live long enough to make them all.

5. Be detached from desire your whole life.

In Buddhist teachings, desire creates attachment and attachment distracts us and prevents enlightenment. While Musashi was not particularly religious, it is certain that he was aware of Buddhism and its tenets. This bit of advice is almost certainly influenced by this exposure to Buddhism.

All desire will be an off-ramp on the highway to your goals and responsibilities. It is natural to feel flattered when someone is flirting with you, but if you are married, you have an obligation to your Wife and to your home. You can feel flattered, but it has to end there. Do not let a moment of feeling good or different or wanted cause you to ruin your home life, your marriage, and even the lives of your children.

Being a man who lives by a code means that there

will be certain sacrifices that we must make. Make them.

Do it right.

If you are going to be attached, and attachment is highly likely in our time, become attached to your goals, or your family. Make it something that matters. Attachment to an object, like the latest tech gadget is just shallow and unbecoming a man of purpose.

6. *Do not regret your actions.*

Everyone has regrets, this is simply a fact of life. But if you make well thought-out decisions, you will minimize your regrets. Impulsivity is a pretty solid indicator of regrets to come.

And if you are doing things now that you know you are not supposed to do or that you know are not good for you, stop doing them. This is not meant to over-simplify the issue, but if you know it is something you should not be doing, then why in the hell are you doing it?

At its base, regret is useful. We all make mistakes, and those of us with a conscience will regret our mistakes. That feeling of regret is there to remind us to not be so foolish again.

We do ourselves and those we love an incredible

disservice when we make mistakes, say we are sorry, and just do the same thing again.

We are supposed to learn from our mistakes and improve ourselves as a result. Otherwise the mistake is just wasted time and energy.

And in case you forgot, you don't have that much time. You are going to make mistakes, accept it. Regret your mistakes, but use that regret as a motivator. In this way you can be sure to grow from it and become a better man as a result.

7. Never be jealous.

All jealousy starts with a lack of appreciation for the good things you have in your own life. If you flip the script and start with appreciation, jealousy is defeated before it takes root in your life.

It is only too easy to look around and see people who are better off than you are. It takes a bit more introspection and observation to look around and see that you have more than others. Even a simple reminder that someone out there is happier than you are with less than you have can help you to see that jealousy is a waste of time and energy.

And we cannot forget that jealousy is a root cause of violence. People talk about poverty as being a cause of violence, but I can say truthfully that I grew up in poverty that you would not believe, and yet I was not violent over it.

It isn't that one person has a mansion and another lives in a tin shoebox in the sun that causes violence, but rather, when the person living in the tin shoebox gets jealous, resentful, and ultimately angry at the person living in the mansion, that violence becomes an option to the poor person.

A poor person who manages to still be happy and content will not ever resort to violence. Contentment *is* wealth. If your happiness isn't rooted in having what others have, you will be better off.

8. Never be saddened by a separation.

Not feeling sadness over loss is impossible. There is no way around it. What is to be done is to go *with* it. You cannot go against it, or psyche is simply not designed to work that way.

Just as with sailing, you need to always keep the wind in your sails. If you find yourself in a need to go against the wind, then tack. But you must *use* the wind.

In rafting, the current is going to take you downriver, on this you have no choice, so it is best to simply go with it

If you fell into a swiftly moving river, you will

wear yourself out trying to swim upstream, and you will still be carried away regardless. If you needed to get out of the river, ride the current and swim to the edge.

Emotions are the same, you have to go with them, and use them to get where you are going safely.

I lost my son. When he passed away, I was a wreck, but I still had responsibilities to my Wife and my Daughters. I had to set aside my grief and do what needed to be done to take care of my Family in those dark times. There is no healing from some separations and losses, but what can be done, and what *must* be done, is to fulfill our obligations.

9. Resentment and complaint are appropriate neither for oneself nor others.

When we are resentful of someone, it usually boils down to feeling that they have things easier than we do. Maybe we are convinced we would be as successful if only we had received the same breaks in life that they had.

But is that really the case or are we making up excuses for our own lack of effort?

Quite often, we fail to see the effort behind the scenes that the other person has put in toward securing their success. Rather than being resentful of another person, be happy for their success. Their success neither picks your pocket nor breaks your bones, so let them enjoy it and allow their success to create no negative energy in your mind.

As for complaint, it is often seen by others as whining.

Are you actively trying to make other people feel sorry for you?

If yes, why? If no, then stop complaining.

Your complaints will often be interpreted as sympathy seeking action, and this is not a good image to give of yourself as a man.

10. Do not let yourself be guided by feelings of lust or love.

Men are hardwired to appreciate the visual. We are not programmed to memorize every detail, but we *are* attuned to notice beauty. This can cause problems in our personal life if we are not in control of ourselves. As such, this is really sound advice from Musashi.

When you notice a beautiful woman, do not obsess. Notice and move on with your day. It is impossible for men to *not* notice beauty, but it is entirely possible to notice, and even appreciate without staring.

Especially for men who are in a committed relationship, or a marriage, or a family life – do not allow the mind to fixate on an object of beauty and turn it into lust. You cannot improve your life or that of your Family if you cannot prioritize them. You will end up being controlled by lust.

Your only controlling influences should be your goals and your commitments. These will be defined by what roles you take on in life. If you are a husband and a Father, take it seriously. Allowing fleeting attractions to destroy your family is something not likely to be easy to recover from, and the damage to the lives of your Wife and your children is likely irreparable.

11. In all things have no preferences.

Going into anything with a preference means your mind is already made up. A closed mind cannot learn, experiences will be limited, and much will be missed.

Obviously, we all prefer certain things. But if we follow this idea, we will be able to be in less than perfect circumstances and still have that undisturbed mind that we seek.

Training yourself to not be controlled by unexamined preferences is really pretty simple. Once in a while, order something completely different in your favorite restaurant. Or try a new kind of coffee.

Read a book from a different genre than what you typically choose.

If you typically fly on vacations, take a road trip or a train instead, for the experience and the freshness of a new experience.

People tend to get stuck because people really are creatures of habit. But we are not *bound*. We can choose what we do, and exploring outside of our normal preferences (within reason), is a good thing in that it expands the range of experiences we are able to draw from in our worldview and decision-making process.

12. Be indifferent to where you live.

Every man has a different station in life, and with that, a different income. Some men live in an apartment, others in a mansion. Some men are homeless.

A man of purpose will not be concerned about how his home compares with that of others. The focus is on the goal, and the goal is to live by your code.

If you do not like where you live, and if it is within your means to do so, make the necessary change. But there are times when you need to stop and appreciate what you have.

Taking this precept further, you might end up with a job that requires you to relocate to an area that you are unfamiliar with. You would need to decide whether or not to take the job. Not taking the job can having a negative impact on your finances and your ability to take care of your family, and it can also lower your worth to the employer. Being indifferent to the precise *where* that you live will allow you to simply go where you need to go for your job, and by extension, for the goal of taking care of your family.

So, yes. Be indifferent to where you live. Make the most of what you have where you are, and do not ever underappreciate how well off you are. But should it become necessary to move elsewhere, be ready and willing to do just that.

13. Do not pursue the taste of good food.

Food, like anything else that crosses the line into obsession and thus becomes a vice, is a balancing act.

Do we live to eat, or do we eat to live?

There are people who choose the path of eating only what is nutritious. There are others who eat whatever the hell they want. When viewed as a whole, there are people from both groups who live longer, and people from each group who die young.

Eat what you want, either path is fine. But eat in moderation. Do not dig your grave with your own fork and spoon. Food can become an obsession and kill you if you are not careful.

Speaking as a person who was once controlled by food cravings, I can tell you from experience and field testing, uncontrolled food worship leads your health to bad places. Many did not survive the gastronomic adventures I participated in, and there is a reason for that.

We are built to survive hunger, not feast. Our bodies can do okay on limited food, but not on unlimited all-you-can-eat.

Choose to be careful and keep an eye on your eating habits.

14. Do not hold on to possessions you no longer need.

Nostalgia is a human trait. And there is nothing wrong with having tokens by which you may remember the past. Photographs, some memorabilia, and other such items are normal to hang on to. Perhaps you have possessions that belonged to a parent who is no longer alive. These have a personal value that is hard to describe. These things can be kept without feeling the need to justify or explain.

But the lesson here is to avoid letting these possessions possess you. After a certain point, some things are no longer necessary.

That taekwondo trophy you got for showing up for your second lesson when you were five years old?

That can probably go.

Some things do not need to accumulate.

There is a tremendous difference between items which are keepsakes and have a sentimental value, and items which you are keeping for no real reason. There is a difference between collecting and hoarding.

It is useful to be able to discern which things are useful and which are not.

15. Do not act following customary beliefs.

In our time we can look at this as following what the latest trend is. And here again, we find the warrior belief that one must not be controlled by unnecessary whims, for this is all that trends are now – the whim of the moment, shared through social media and practiced by people who find their true self to be unbearably dull.

A better response to finding your true self to be too dull to face is to *actually* change your true self. You can become better than you are now.

It is incredibly easy to simply run with the crowd and do what they do. Look at the ease with which people are able to do the most asinine things, often with no other reason than that other people are doing it.

And in a certain way, this advice falls into the same category as the words of Socrates when he said that the unexamined life is not worth living.

If you are going to act a certain way, there should be a reason for doing so.

Sometimes a man has to buck the tide. It is a definite character flaw to follow every latest behavioral trend one sees on social media. Understand why you are doing what you do, and in the long run you will be happier as a result.

16. Do not collect weapons or practice with weapons beyond what is useful.

There are those who argue that staff, sword, and spear are obsolete, and therefore anyone who trains in their use is wasting their time.

People also think the Kentucky Long Rifle is obsolete. However, the Kentucky Long Rifle will blow a golf ball sized hole in a person. Since most people in this country are not fighting in a war zone, when a home invader suddenly turns up with a massive hole in his torso, the inability to reload quickly is irrelevant. Useful depends on a lot of variables.

It is a good thing to be familiar with the practical usage of many weapons. It is a bad thing to have no specialty.

A man should have some fighting expertise. It can be striking, grappling, edged weapons, blunt weapons, firearms, polearms, or anything else. But one must have an area where there is a supreme confidence and skill.

Know how to use any weapon you keep in your home. If you own weapons right now that you do not know how to use, get some training! A surface knowledge of several weapons does no harm, provided you have something where your knowledge is deep.

17. Do not fear death.

A man who fears death will find death everywhere.

Everyone dies, no matter their diet, exercise routine, or how careful or protected they are. Humans are simply not built for more than seven decades, and even when survive that long we are typically miserable.

Live. The shadow of death is everywhere, but a man must not quake in fear of it. We are genetically predisposed to sacrificing our lives when the need arises.

In times past, men knew that we were expendable. We knew and accepted this fact. It shaped a lot of our views and was an emphasis on the importance of training in ways to make us capable of facing our own mortality without being controlled by fear.

You are going to die. Everyone you know is going to die. Everyone you have ever met or even heard of is going to die. You cannot escape this fact through money, or power, or bargaining, or sex, or drugs, or alcohol.

Even being afraid will not add a minute to your life.

What a waste and a shame to tremble in fear when death is not even knocking at the door! When the moment comes, it comes. Until then, live!

18. Do not seek to possess goods or fiefs for your old age.

If you are truly walking life's path alone, then this

advice is right up your alley. If you have a Wife and children, then you need to consider providing for them when death has taken you away.

In the days of warriors who died young, what need would they have of goods and property in old age which they would never see? That context is important!

For our time and our purposes here, we can say that one should not be distracted by the acquisition of material things. A more expensive car will not make your kid into a better person. Making more money than others will only earn the respect of sycophants.

The real focus of a man's life should be on being the best man that he can be. That is where we can have a lasting effect on the world. Our name and our reputation is what lives on after we are gone.

In our time, planning for our old age is called "being responsible". It is something we should all do. But, as men who understand that we are expendable, we should also consider what value we bring to our family after we are gone. What will our name and reputation do for our children and our wife when we are no longer here? Will our reputation be so strong that those who speak ill of us are simply dismissed without thought, or will they be believed?

19. Respect Buddha and the gods without counting on their help.

If you are a religious person, there is nothing wrong with it, and there is nothing about it that lessens your masculinity.

If you are atheist, there is nothing wrong with that, and nothing about it that lessens your masculinity.

This is not about religion, but about practicality.

You can use religion as a guide, and as a help in finding and establishing the precepts of your personal code of conduct. But in a moment of crisis, in physical conflict, you must act and not wait for divine intervention.

If, after the event has passed, you look at the way things played out and you find signs of the hand of God, that's fine. But when it is time to act, you must act and not wait.

There are those who insist that every moment is preordained by the very hand of God. But others look at the rivers of blood spilled by those who believed in a fervent hope that God would save them from death, and say that their faith was meaningless. No one knows the real answer.

You can be true to your beliefs and still defend

your life.

20. You may abandon your own body, but you must preserve your honor.

As stated earlier, we all die. What lives on is our legacy, the way we will be remembered by those who knew us, or in some cases, those who have heard of us.

Avoid doing those things that you would not want posted on social media on the day you die.

People in our time relish the chance to destroy another person's reputation, especially once that person is dead and cannot say anything in their own defense. Protect your honor because that is all that you will have standing in your defense when you are gone.

In America, the concept of honor is very vague. And the fear of death is immense.

If we can understand the importance of living in such a way that we are remembered in a good way when we are gone, we will act in ways that benefit those around us.

Understanding that the body is less important in the overall scheme of things than our honor, we will be able to place our focus on the important things. And in finding this better focus, we will be able to have a bigger and more lasting impact on the world around us.

21. Never stray from the way.

While Musashi is referring to *the way of the* warrior when he uses the term "the way", for our purposes here, we can look at the *Way* as being our code of conduct, the way of being a man.

So, if within your code of manhood you say that your need to respect the honor of women, then you need to live in such a way that you do not disrespect women.

If your code of manhood includes precepts about being a real Father to your children, then you need to be present and there for your kids. You cannot shirk this responsibility and still claim that you are being are real man by your own standards. Live up to what you claim to be, and in doing so you can be sure that you are worthy of the blood shed by your Fathers.

A code of conduct is useless if you do not follow it. There may be distractions and temptations, but a man must keep an eye on his responsibilities and honor those first. If these are tied directly into your personal code, then you will be able to stick to the way through being a grown ass man and owning your responsibilities.

Do not ever abandon your code or you will lose more than you ever think you could gain from the distraction.

Notes: Musashi was a warrior in a time of warriors.

He was also a little bit nuts.

Setting aside his mental health, if only half of the stories about him are true, he was a genuine badass.

He was not writing these precepts for our time. He was writing for his student, who was also a warrior. The thought that people would still be reading his words this long after his death probably never entered his mind. We are lucky to still have his teachings.

The warrior cultures still hold much value for our modern men. Musashi was most certainly a man's man. From his writing we can see that sometimes a man has to make hard decisions. Sometimes a man is going to have to sacrifice the easy and fun for the harder path. Take this to heart. Sacrifice is an essential ingredient in being true to your code as a man.

Sometimes we do not want to sacrifice for others. But if we are to be a real man, there is a lot we have to do that is less fun than some of the other things we can be doing.

Being a good man isn't always easy, but it has its own rewards. There is nothing better or more fulfilling than to watch your child grow up and start to forge their own place in the world. Your own parents could have had a better life, financially speaking, but they opted to raise you. People used to live as an example for their children, but somewhere along the way too many people stopped seeing this point.

There are many other examples that could be used to demonstrate a man's sacrifice, but the point is made already. Do the right thing, even when it isn't the easy thing.

5 Cowboy Wisdom

Category: General Badass
Origin: American West (The Wild West for those of
you not from Texas)

As people migrated to the American west to settle and establish towns and lives, there grew a different breed of man, the Cowboy.

Most people only know of the cowboy of movie and TV legend. Most of what people know as fact incorrect.

The actual start of the Cowboy has its roots in Spain and the cattle ranch method that was brought from Spain to the Americas.

In America, the original cowboys were actually

outlaws. They were people who decided that how they lived and what they did was up to them. They did not recognize any laws or lawmakers.

But to most people, when they think of Cowboys, what they really picture is the old west gunslingers.

We have images in mind of two men standing face to face waiting for the other to make the first move, and then we will see which one was faster.

In reality, gunfights in the old west were typically more spontaneous.

Imagine an argument where suddenly one person draws a gun, the other person could only react. This was the common situation of the old west gunfight. The Hollywood version may have happened at times, and it is historical fact that duels existed. But to believe that things always played out in the movie style is silly.

But the old west did have a code of conduct of sorts. There are very few stories of well-known gunslingers in a shootout with each other. The fast-draw types tended to avoid confrontation with one another, each probably knowing that their reputation exceeded their true capabilities, and they also wished to not tempt fate too often.

Most of the trouble was caused by a lesser known

person trying to establish a reputation by being the one who took out the more famous person.

One such incident that comes to mind is when Jack McCall shot Wild Bill Hickok in the back of the head as he played cards.

Wild Bill was very well known and his speed and accuracy were the stuff of legend. On August 2, 1876, Jack McCall took the only advantage he was likely to find, and went down in the history books as the man who killed Wild Bill[5].

Over time, the definition of Cowboy morphed into the all American tough guy; gun-toting, self-reliant, hard-working and fiercely independent. The American spirit is writ large in the Cowboy ways.

The list that follows comes from public domain, and the thoughts that follow each precept are my own.

Live each day with courage.

A man cannot spend his days in fear of what might happen. Everyone has good days and bad days. Sometimes things go your way, and other

---

[5] McCall was found *Not Guilty* in a trial held in Deadwood shortly after the murder. Although there are laws against Double Jeopardy, he was tried a second time in Yankton, and the second trial was allowed and McCall was found guilty and was executed on March 1, 1877, at the age of 24.

times they go all wrong. What are you supposed to do then?

Face it.

Enjoy the good days, they are few and far between for most people. Soak them in and savor those days. Face the bad days. There are plenty of them. So many, in fact, that if you try to hide from them you will often find the next day will be worse.

Don't spend your days in fear. Face each day ready and willing to tackle whatever comes your way.

Take pride in your work.

Anything worth the time it takes you to do, is worth doing right. This is where taking pride in your work begins. Because the work is done by you, it is tied forever to your name, you should make it as perfect as possible.

There are many easy examples in our time of people who have no pride in what they do, from private contractors to professional athletes, there is no shortage of people who feel entitled to success without effort.

A man must put in the effort if he is to be successful. If you have pride in what you do, then success will come as a result of your own effort, and your pride in your work will easily increase.

Always finish what you start.

This is the follow-through that is part and parcel of success. Being strong in the beginning is easy. Being strong as you carry the heavy load over a long distance is another matter entirely.

Finishing what you start is about dedication. It is also tied to taking pride in your work. A man is not supposed to do anything half-assed. Whatever it is that you do, you should see it through from start to finish.

Whether it is a project at work or raising your kids, you *follow-through*. You see it through to the end of your responsibilities (which, in the case of your kids, never really ends).

Do what has to be done.

There are things that no one *wants* to do. Washing dishes, doing laundry, changing diapers – no one has ever looked forward to these tasks. But they have to be done. Add in going to work when you don't feel like it. What about owning up to your choices and taking care of your responsibilities? The list keeps on growing.

Doing what has to be done is a sign of maturity. A child will play video games all day even when they have homework to do. A child will lay around doing nothing rather than taking care of chores. Are you a man or a child?

In a larger sense, doing what needs to be done as a man means owning the responsibility to provide for your family and to defend those under your care. Take these roles to heart and live them out fully.

Be tough, but fair.

Being a hardass to everyone is not a sign of manhood, it is a sign of insecurity. It is not possible to treat everyone equally, but it is a simple matter to treat people fairly. To be a man of quality, one must have a sense of equity. To be fair means to repay kindness with kindness, but to repay unkindness with justice.

People often overlook the Biblical saying of *an eye for an eye* as being a limiting law. At the time those words entered Hebrew law, if a person took your eye out, it was not unheard of to annihilate their entire family from the face of the earth.

Being tough must carry with it the limitations of being fair, or else you will become a tyrant and a bully.

You can be tough and yet fair.

When you make a promise, keep it.

A lesson lost on politicians.

When you make a promise, you are giving your

word, and with that your honor, to fulfill what you say you will do. When you promise but fail to act, you damage your reputation and are rightfully seen as a liar.

Such reputations are very hard to change.

This is not to say it will be easy to just keep your promises; it isn't easy at all. This is one reason why it is a good idea to not promise anything that you are not sure you can deliver.

Keep in mind that there are times when all a person has to base a decision about you on is your reputation. Make your word mean something, or there will be consequences down the road.

Ride for the brand.

This expression means loyalty to one's employer. When you feed your family through working for another person or company, you should treat that company fairly. It is poor form to work for a company and spend your time bad-mouthing or running the company down. Employers invest time and money in employees, and they rightfully expect a modest amount of loyalty in return.

Do what is right. If you feel you are unappreciated or not being treated right, move on. But do not speak ill of them. When you go to a job interview for a new position, talking down a former employer may feel good, but it hurts your chances of being hired by the new company, because they feel that you may do the same to them if you end up feeling discontent with your new job.

And they are probably right in their assumption.

Be better than that.

Talk less and say more.

There are people who love to hear themselves speak.

These are the people in a meeting who will say things that have no connection to the topic or task at hand.

It is better, more often than not, to hold your tongue and just listen.

You will find that many people in a meeting or place of business miss a lot of what is said in meetings because they are waiting for a time to interject their own thoughts, or else they are trying to come up with a response to what is being said at that moment.

In *Texas Hold'em Self-Defense*, I made reference to a genetic survival code – one mouth and two ears. Listen more than you speak.

In addition to saying less it is equally important to say things that matter. It is easy to engage in small talk, but it is not enlightening.

When you listen more than you speak, you learn. You become patient, and this patience allows you to take the time needed to create an informed opinion and formulate a way to express it that will have the best impact on the listener.

There is no downside to this.

Some things aren't for sale.

It is okay to sell your labor. Most of us work for someone else, and this is a fact of the world we live in. There is no shame and no harm in this.

Some people sell ideas. Inventors may create a new thingy of some type or another, and sell the patent (the idea, for all intents and purposes), and this too is respectable.

A man should not sell his name. A man should not sell his family. And a man must not sell his reputation.

Selling your name would involve allowing people to use your name and likeness without your input. If you develop a reputation in your field, you need to keep control of your name. You should never allow yourself to be put into a position where you cannot take your name and reputation and move on if you wish.

Selling your family would involve allowing work or fame to ruin your home life. If your work takes you away from home so much that your home life is falling apart, then you are failing in several aspects of being a man.

Selling your reputation is related in that if you allow work to bring you to a point of breaking faith or bringing dishonor to you or your family, you are making a tremendous mistake.

Know where to draw the line.

Just as a man has to have a code to live by, a man has to have limits. Knowing where to draw the line means just that.

People treat you the way that they do based on two things; what you allow, and what you encourage.

Many men allow themselves to be treated any way that another person chooses, for whatever reason.

This is a shame because it sets a standard of how you will be treated from that time on. If you do not draw the line, you set yourself up for long-term misery in that you have set a baseline standard level of treatment that the other person will believe is okay with you. Leave the suffering saint routine for the actual saints.

Other men take this a step further and actually encourage their own mistreatment. This is even worse than the first situation because you reward the person who is doing the mistreatment.

It is best to stop these issues when they are small and before they fester into something truly problematic. This involves being a man and speaking up. For some men this isn't easy, but for all men, it is absolutely necessary. Is it really worth it in the long run, to allow yourself to be treated like garbage by anyone in the hope that they will like you more? Or is it a hope for sex? Grow up.

Notes: From the American west, we can see many traditional beliefs and customs that fit right in to a man's code of ethics.

Sometimes, being a man and doing the right thing are not the easiest things, but if you are a man, you might as well do it right. Being a cowboy in our modern age will certainly make you stand out in a crowd, but when you look at the crowd that you are standing out from, you have to ask – is standing out such a bad thing?

While it is easy to look at the modern version of the American Old West and its Cowboys and simply write it off as romanticism, there are many points we need to consider.

For a start, the people who settled the west were extremely mentally tough. They left everything they had and everything they knew to settle in rough areas without cities and the comforts of home. They were in danger of death by starvation, Indian attacks, drought, snakebite, disease, and bad water.

They went anyway.

They stayed anyway.

How often do we see people in our time who never even try to do things just because the trying might be hard?

We can be so much more than that, and we should be. We must not forget that we come from tough stock. Our forefathers we tough as nails and simply did what had to be done, often for no other reason than it had to be done. And they did this without the benefit of modern technology, which allows us to find any information we need within seconds.

We can and we should be keeping their example in the front of our minds. We can be as tough as our Fathers, and we can do as much, if we are willing to get in and do the work needed.

6 Gichin Funakoshi's 20 Precepts

Category: General Badass
Origin: Japan

Probably the most famous of the Okinawan karate masters to bring the art to Japan was Gichin Funakoshi. His writings remain standard teaching in most of the karate world to this day.

He was born in 1868, and entered the world fighting for his life, being born prematurely in a time and place where such things did not bode well.

He began training in karate as a child. Far from being only a karate master, his studies were broad and he was a school teacher in Okinawa.

His karate training was in the schools of Shorei-ryu and Shorin-ryu. He founded the Shotokan school, Shotokan meaning "*House of Shoto*". Shoto was Funakoshi's pen name.

It was Funakoshi who changed the written name of Karate from *China hand* (唐手) to *empty hand* (空手)[6].

The original term gives us the origin of the art, while the later was designed to allow a national pride in the system which had admittedly changed drastically from its Chinese roots.

While he was a very small man in stature, one would be hard pressed to find anyone who could say the Funakoshi was not a badass man. He was a true master of the art of the empty hand. While his precepts had more to do with martial arts and martial artists, they are included here as they provide some strong advice that applies directly

---

[6] Although completely different in pictographic writing, both versions are pronounced the same, "kara te".

toward being a good man.

He published several books, and in his autobiography, *Karate-do, My Way of Life,* he gave us his 20 precepts of karate. The 20 precepts set out by Gichin Funakoshi probably predate him and his work. However, as they are most widely known as his work, they are present them here as such.

Karate begin and ends with courtesy.

In many martial arts systems, the training sets, called *kata*, begin and end with a bow. The bow is not to be viewed as just part of the form. There is a deeper meaning. It is an outward display of respect by the trainee to the art and those who teach it.

For a man, being courteous and respectful should be second nature. Common (or should it be called uncommon?) courtesy can keep you out of harm's way even when you travel into unfamiliar territory with rules and norms that may be far removed from your own experiences.

Getting into the habit of being courteous to everyone will not only keep you safe, it will bring about a response of respect from most people.

In a situation that is tense, try courtesy first. You might be surprised at the results.

There is no first attack in karate.

This means that one is not to go out in search of a fight. Trouble comes often and easily enough without going out of your way to find it. There is no cause to be the first to attack, aside from being absolutely certain that you are about to be attacked.

In a deeper way, we can also look at this as not being a jerk. It is the lower class person who is a hardass to everyone and finds a reason to be offended by everything imaginable. There is no justification for such attitudes and behaviors to a grown man.

Karate is an aid to justice.

A man should be able to carry himself in a fight.

However, developing our ability in the field of fighting does not give us permission to fight without a just cause.

There are times when a man not only is justified in fighting, but is actually *obligated* to fight. When it comes to protecting women and children from violence, there should be no other consideration. A man must do what is right. If that means using violence to protect others, then so be it.

The previous statement is not politically correct in our time, but this does not make the statement *incorrect.*

We are the protectors. We have *always* been the protectors. Societal trends and politically correct BS do not excuse us from fulfilling these obligations.

If you are to be a good man, then you need to be a just man. Do what is right, whether what is right comes easy or not.

Karate is an aid to justice, for us and for our purposes here means that *men* are an aid to justice.

First control yourself before attempting to control others.

In our time it is disturbingly common to think that you must force others into your way of thinking. People are overly quick to offer their opinions on how others should live, but very slow to look at how they themselves live, or even notice how they fail to live up to their professed ideologies.

A man must understand first that he lives his own life, and *only* his own life. You are only qualified to make the decisions that affect your life. Other people have to live their own life and must make their own decisions, and reap the benefits or face the consequences, whichever the case may be.

Since it is impossible to force others to live the way you say, it is a simple choice to live your own life to the best of your knowledge.

Spirit first, technique second.

Obviously, this is a martial arts advice, but it does apply to anyone outside of martial arts as well when viewed correctly.

Spirit first and technique second in the martial arts applies to the energy, the fighting spirit which animates the martial arts. This energy is a force of will, and it is more important than individual techniques. It is the same thing that I tell my students all of the time. I say, "I can teach you all of the techniques in the world, but if you don't supply the heart, then you are going to be terrible."

When applying this to non-martial areas of life, look toward what you do to provide for your family.

Whatever the job is and whatever station in life you feel is attached to the status associated with that station, go in every single day and be the best person for the job that you can be. Give it your all and never do it half-assed.

Let the spirit of your honor to your duty energize your work and the effort you put in toward taking care of your obligations in life.

Good things can come your way from simply

being productive at work. When you place the spirit of the work ahead of the mundane view of the individual tasks you perform each day, then you will breathe new life into yourself and into the work that you do.

Especially if you have a family, do your dead level best every day. Take pride in being able *and willing* to take care of your Family. This is the man's job and task in this life. Do it, to the best of your ability, and you will find a great pride in your work.

Always be ready to release your mind.

For our purposes here, this applies to being able to concentrate on the task at hand. There are worries and concerns enough to carry the day and keep us wrapped up in a little cocoon of self-pity.

We don't want to be like that.

We need to be better than that, and it is fairly easy to do if we learn to concentrate on what we are doing right now.

Our work might be tedious and the hours long. But we can do better by maintaining our focus in the moment. On the plus side, our work will come out much better, and the time will pass faster.

Accidents arise from negligence.

We have all experienced a moment where an accident of one type or another occurred in a moment where we were simply not paying attention. We feel stupid and kick ourselves over it repeatedly.

And we *should* feel stupid over things like this. Through the simple act of paying attention, we could have avoided the entire incident.

What is called for is to make focus a habit.

Start right now. If there is a noise in the room where you are, see if you can focus on hearing it enough that other noises from outside seem to disappear. Or turn on the TV and the radio, and try to only hear one or the other through focus. This simple task can allow you to see how easy it is to focus on one thing.

If you can do it, you can focus on any task if you simply choose to do so.

Do not think karate training is only in the dojo.

For a martial artist, to ever think that their only training occurs in the *dojo* (training hall) is absurd.

For training to reach any of the higher levels, your actions *outside* of the training hall need to be a reflection or a continuation of the lessons from *inside* the training hall.

For a non-martial artist, simply begin to look at each facet of your life as an extension or continuation of the main part of your life.

If your family is the center of your life, then view your work as the means by which you provide for your family.

Look at taking care of your health as the way you ensure that you are *able* to work to take care of your family.

Teach yourself to keep the center of your life as the center, and you will find that many other things fall into place more easily.

It will take your entire life to learn karate, there is no limit.

A man can study martial arts for his entire life and find new things to learn every day. All it takes for this to occur is a beginner's mindset. If you ever reach a point where you feel that you know everything, you will not only stop learning, you will stagnate and then regress.

Outside of the martial arts, the same rule applies.

Whatever it is that you do, you should approach it with a beginner's mind.

There is a lot to learn in this world, and the truth is that you will not live long enough to learn it all.

Whatever the field of study you choose, never stop learning, never declare yourself to be a master of any system, style, or field of study. Remain a student and you will never reach a point where you are left behind by those with a better approach.

The best teachers are forever students, but they are different because they are students who cannot help but share with others what they have learned. They have a passion for what they study that prevents them from *not* telling others about it.

Put your everyday living into karate and you will find subtle secrets.

In martial arts and in life, if you pay attention you will find an interconnectedness in many aspects of your life. Many miracles are overlooked and unnoticed simply because we are not paying attention.

Throw yourself fully into living your life, not for tomorrow or next week, but see what is happening *right now*.

Always keep your mind in the now and these things will become clearer and clearer.

Karate is like boiling water; if you do not heat it constantly, it will cool.

As a skill, karate must be practiced constantly.

Any skills or aspects of the art that a practitioner fails to train, over time will disappear. The trainee must practice daily, and must practice intensely.

So too, all aspects of manhood must be put into practice or they will disappear for you. If you think that one aspect is less important than another, you will fail to be all that you can be. You will fall short.

Vigilance is key. Keep an eye out for any excuses you are making for slacking off. As soon as you see this happening, exercise some discipline and refocus on your goals and responsibilities.

Discipline will carry you through when natural skills might not. You cannot rely on always being the strongest or smartest. Being the most disciplined will really set you apart.

Do not focus on winning, focus on not losing.

The difference between the two is subtle. When your focus is on winning, you will be constantly seeking an edge over everyone. You will be seeking their defeat, and this will have a profound negative impact on everyone around you.

There is absolutely nothing wrong with being competitive, it is in truth an important part of being a man. But some things can end up being taken to the extreme.

When you shift your focus toward not losing, you can be strong, and still very competitive, but you will be a lot less of a hooplehead to the people around you. You will maintain that masculine competitiveness, but you will not make those around you miserable.

A focus on not losing will allow you to center your attention on training mind and body to make yourself unassailable.

Victory depends on being able to distinguish between vulnerable and invulnerable points.

In your life, there will be conflict.

This is especially so in our time if you choose to pursue the road of recovering your masculinity. There will be name calling, terms like sexist and misogynist will be used quite liberally.

You will need to suffer the insults as best you can, and defend when necessary.

Defending against slander is challenging. You want to counter the insult, and yet you do not want to be seen as the evil one, and you certainly do not want to be seen as confirming their worst defamatory accusations.

The vulnerable point of the verbal slanderer is logic and truth. Obviously, the accuser will not see it. Because of the overwhelming number of modern youth who have never been taught to properly argue, they will use cheap tactics like misquoting you and attacking what they falsely accuse you of saying.

Rise above. You will not convince them, but you *can* convince those who are watching. It may seem like there is no one left out there who can still use logic and reason, but they are there and they are numerous, this is not always obvious because they are also quiet. Have faith that this course is the right course and follow through. All shall be well.

Know when to fight, and know where your adversary is vulnerable. When you hit back, hit them twice as hard as they had hit you, but hit them where they are vulnerable.

The fight depends on how you move.

There is a saying in the martial arts, "make your opponent fight *your* fight". You achieve this by forcing your opponent to move into positions that *you* choose for him.

An easy example is that if you want him to drop his hands, start attacking low. When he drops his hands to defend, you will attack high, which was your intention all along.

A man must know how to bring an adversary into a vulnerable position. This is done sometimes by appearing to be unguarded, and at other times by appearing to be protecting a certain position, or stating a desired end that you have no intention of securing.

In doing this, you force the adversary to take positions or try to block certain outcomes when all along you had another endgame in mind. In fighting, deception is key.

Think of your hands and feet as swords.

This is, obviously, applied to the martial art of karate, whose very name means *empty hands*. When you fight without weapons, you need to improvise.

When swords are outlawed, you must make your hands and feet into swords.

For what we are trying to achieve here, we can look at this precept as meaning that a man should never view himself as ever being truly disarmed.

Maybe you are good with a gun, but your work forces you to travel to a very prohibitive area. You can do the macho-dumbass thing and carry your gun anyway, opening yourself up to prison time and a loss of legal gun ownership. Or, alternatively, you could follow the local laws, but view your body as a weapon.

Because the traditional role of a man involves protecting others, he *must* train to fight, and must be (at the very least) moderately proficient with grappling, fist, foot, blade, and gun.

There is nothing wrong having a specialty, in fact we all should. But having a working knowledge of every range makes a man best equipped to fulfill that role as protector.

When you go outside, think of attackers everywhere.

In self-defense classes there is a common line about staying aware of your surroundings. It is taught that one should be aware of at least two possible escape routes, location of fire extinguishers, options for cover and for concealment[7] if cover is unavailable, etc.

For what we are doing, look at this advice to be about the practice of visualization.

Visualization is nothing magical, it is simply an act of anticipation. When you are going up for a promotion at work, think about the possible questions and what your answers might be.

If there is an argument coming and you know it is going to happen, think about how it might go ahead of time. Anticipate how you might be attacked, and what your best response might be.

---

[7] For those who do not know the difference between cover and concealment; cover is a barrier that will stop a bullet, and concealment is a barrier that prevents the enemy from seeing you.

Do not try for the wittiest comeback, but do consider options on how to best state your position.

This is not to say you will have a superpower that allows you to see the future and control it. But rather, it is to say that by considering all possibilities, you have a chance to anticipate different events and have time to prepare to respond to them constructively.

Beginners use stances, advanced practitioners use posture.

Regardless of your personal field of study, if you are advanced in the field, there are things that you do radically different than what you did as a beginner.

In the martial arts, beginners are taught how to stand and transition from one stance (a way of standing) to another stance.

This training teaches the neophyte to move their bodyweight in the proper way without the unnecessary cumbersome questions from the trainee about *what is my bodyweight and how do I move it?*

When you are a beginner you must use the tools given to beginners by those who have gone before you. When you are advanced, you must discard these training wheels for the more advanced interpretations of what you are doing.

This advice is about knowing your station in your field of study. Learn it well.

Kata is one thing, a real fight is another.

In the martial arts, *kata* are sets of movements performed in a predesigned order that mimic a fight. They are a textbook for the style or system being taught.

Kata is clean, neat, and orderly.

Fighting is another beast entirely.

Fighting is ugly, dirty, and is not limited. Fighting might involve a thumb in the eye, yours or his.

Fighting carries the risk of death or permanent injury. Fighting is also a *Go Directly to Jail, Do Not Pass Go, Do not collect $200* card, as well as courts, lawyers, and all that goes along with that.

Outside of the martial arts, one might view this advice as telling you to never mistake the map for the terrain.

What you learn in your textbook is not useless, but it is also not the real world. When you study in preparation for your work, what you are learning is the codified bits of information that has been deemed important by those who have been there.

However, the real world is a lot more fluid and wiggly than your teachers can ever put into writing.

The textbooks are tools, and they are there to give you basic information, a point of departure, if you will. The actual terrain is going to have all kinds of surprises and you need to be ready for that, rather than feeling a shock that *they never told me about this!*

Hard and soft, tension and relaxation, quick and slow, all connected in the technique.

Because this is not directly a book about martial arts, we will not go into the real depth of what is being said here to a martial artist, instead we will keep our thoughts to the intended focus.

There are many different qualities that make up a complete man. It is easy to say this is and that isn't what a man is, but we are not children.

It is much more beneficial to point out that there are many different aspects to manhood.

A man must be violent when protecting his family. But he must be soft when entertaining his daughter. He must be without emotion when at work, or when teaching his son to hunt, but he must express emotion honestly and openly to his

Wife.

There is no *one size fits all* answer when it comes to the emotional state of a man, because we have to be different things at different times.

Be ready and capable for these different situations.

Think of ways to apply these precepts every day.

Like any other code of conduct, these precepts will do you no good at all as long as they remain mere concepts. They must be put into practice, or else they are just a theory.

Notes: Karate teaches its practitioners to forge their hands and feet into weapons that are used (originally) as a replacement for spear and sword. It is in this way that we can adapt a karate mindset in our pursuit of being the best man that we can be.

Karate training takes patience and any real skill is going to be the product of *years*.

Learning to live by a code of manhood is the same.

You will not miraculously become a great man overnight. It is going to take years of working on living the code you choose, making mistakes, resetting, and trying again.

You are not perfect and you never will be, but this does not mean that you cannot be awesome. Do the work, put in the time and the training. Fall down, but get right back up and get back into the fight.

7 *The Roman Republic*

Category: Warrior Culture

Origin: Italy

The Roman Republic, not to be confused with the Roman Empire, began with the overthrow of what is called the Roman Kingdom, and ended with the start of the Roman Empire. During the time of the Roman Republic, Rome's control expanded until it covered the entire Mediterranean civilization.

The Roman Republic was at war for most of its existence. Of note were wars with Gaul, Carthage, and Macedonia.

Roman culture held certain traits in high regard. In this chapter we will examine these traits and look at how we might apply these virtues in our daily life.

Dignitas.

Most commonly translated as dignity, this is a quality that a man develops throughout his entire life.

Dignitas is developed through keeping an eye on your personal reputation, which would involve many of the factors discussed in other chapters. It is closely tied to your morality as viewed by society and your peers. It also directly affects how much respect you are going to receive as a standard treatment by others.

We can call it a *virtue*, which in its original sense was really *manliness*.

For instance, if you are a man who is honest in your business dealings, you should rightly expect others to treat you the same. If you are faithful to your wife and family, you should expect to be treated in kind. If you fulfill your obligations and promises to others, they should feel obligated to do the same for you.

If you guard your honor in your interactions with others, and if you are careful to do what is morally right, you can be sure that you will earn the respect of those around you.

There will always be those who slander you out of jealousy. There are people who are just bad people and they live to treat others poorly.

Let them.

You can only live your life and ensure only your own reputation.

None of this is easy, but as they say; if it were easy, everyone would do it.

Guard your worth, merit, and reputation. You cannot replace them.

And in speaking of dignitas, the great statesman Cicero advised that equality (given so much lip-service in our time), is poor in that it follows the idea of reducing all men to some common denominator, instead advising that those who, through work and development of dignitas, merit more, and should receive more.

We could do well to understand and live this in our time. While so many scream that we should all have an equal outcome, Dignitas calmly states that we should gain only what we earn. Any man worth his salt knows that earning gives a sense of self-worth that entitlement never can.

We shall leave this with one clear thought. Caesar himself noted that his dignitas was dearer to him than life itself. How many in our time can say that?

Auctoritas.

Auctoritas is the root of the word *authority*. Like dignitas, auctoritas has to do with personal reputation, but it has a different focus. This was not mere reputation; auctoritas was the power of command, the ability to gather support for your idea or cause.

It should be obvious that in our time, gaining support does not necessarily mean that what you are doing is right. People these days can gain a tremendous support and following for stupid things like blocking streets or walking outside of their purposely driverless car.

This is about something more.

Leadership is a rare skill. It can be developed, but it requires a rewiring of the brain. Everyone has selfish tendencies. But leaders are able to harness an ability to make those around them better by finding a sense of pride and achievement in the success of those they lead. Leadership, *real* leadership, is never about promoting yourself, it is all about raising the performance of those around you.

Auctoritas is real leadership. And it is sorely

needed in our time. It is not to be confused with the Latin word *potestas*, which means power. Auctoritas is also power, but in every context it seems to mean a power with legitimacy.

When you have auctoritas, you are in control, and not at the mercy of the mob or your personal whim. This is why it is more prized.

How often in our day do we see entire groups of people slip into mob mentality because they are told to do so on social or news media?

The craving for momentary fame, viral posts, and celebrations of ignorance is everywhere. But, this is not a power of any real sort. It is a fleeting moment of being celebrated, not truly being recognized. It is short-term and it is useless. And it most certainly is not power.

Power, real power, will come from auctoritas. Be a leader, develop those skills, and auctoritas will come.

Otium.

Otium is another term that is hard to give an exact definition to in English.

In truth, it has many different translations. It can mean leisure time. It can mean the time one has after retirement, when one is free to pursue the spiritual, the significant, and the contemplative.

The origin of the word is tied to withdrawing from one's work in order to engage in things like public speaking or writing.

If a man lives a full and varied life, accumulating many experiences, he is able to practice otium in sharing those experiences and hard won knowledge with those young minds in his field of expertise, and in so doing help to give those minds a head start which may bring them tremendous success. This is a way of giving back that can give one a lasting legacy in their field.

Alternatively, one may use the time after retirement to pursue matters of spiritual, psychological, or philosophical study. This too is otium. Ones days are never wasted if they are spent in learning.

So, while young, live and learn and study. Then, when the time comes, take your place as an elder statesman, share the knowledge you have accumulated in your years. Be a benefit to the young men around you. Be a guide. Be a mentor.

Be a leader.

Pietas.

Pietas is *devotion to duty*.

It is about paying what is owed, even when what is owed is hard to put into concrete terms. It is also described as being the drive behind the fulfillment of duty. It is that force which *compels* us to do our duty.

Men must possess this quality, or else we would all be those deadbeat dads we read about.

It is our duty to provide for our children and for the mother of our children. It is our sacred responsibility. We cannot complain about this, because it is certain that we really enjoyed making those kids!

Pietas goes further than our paternal obligations. We have obligations in our business relations as well.

If we are an employee, we are expected to be there every day performing our job functions. This is not negotiable, we owe it in the fair exchange of labor for cash. If we are an employer, we are obligated to pay our employees fairly as agreed.

Fulfill your obligations in such a way that people know that you are someone who can be counted on.

Gravitas.

Gravitas was especially important for leaders of

men. Various translations leave us with the general impression that gravitas is a serious dignity, almost meaning *importance*.

Gravitas will be developed over time through the practice of the other virtues.

In our time, if one is to be taken seriously, then one should first give people a reason to take you seriously.

You should be knowledgeable, well-read, honest, and be someone people look to for answers.

This is developed only with time and conscious attention to your conduct and dealings with others. If you are not one to take anything seriously, you will have a hard time in convincing people to take you seriously.

If you *demand* respect, you may or may not get it. If you *command* respect, you will be respected, even when people cannot explain why they respect you.

Notes: Rome was a great experiment in governance, perhaps second only to the American founding in all of history. It was imperfect and had its flaws. But, as a society, it gives us a code of manhood that is outstanding.

We see in the code of the Romans that there is a

cycle to life. They did not ignore the fact that people age and die. In our time we tend to sweep this under the rug.

In your own time, you will make a lot of mistakes when you are young. And if you are aware, these mistakes will each bring you closer to your goals. Each miss will be closer to the mark[8]. When you are older, you can start to forge your role as the elder statesman.

There is no need to fear aging if you are prepared for and understand the changing roles you will have as it happens.

Eventually, if you are one of the lucky ones, you will have the chance to withdraw from your field and pursue those things that you wish to study further with what time you have.

Use your days wisely, and when the time is right, give back to society. In this way, you can make the world a better place.

---

[8] Interestingly, the Greek word for sinning, ἁμαρτάνειν (hamartánein) means "to miss the mark" and it is an archery term. Missing the mark is essentially not hitting the bullseye.

8 Chivalric code

Category: Warrior Culture
Origin: Europe

Any list of the actual "code of chivalry" is going to be argued about by anyone with an opinion and an internet connection.

We have no official list. This is due in large part to the fact that the era of knights and chivalry spanned so much time that different writers of the times wrote differing accounts of what that code of conduct contained.

The oldest of these codes was called the *Noble Habitus* and was essentially a code of conduct for everyone, a societal and behavioral expectation which had been written down, and was intended to be applied to everyone in society.

Certain things such as loyalty were held to be of high importance, and should be prized by any society in the world.

There were also guidelines established regarding a knight's behavior around his superiors. Again, this is standard and should be practiced by all.

In this chapter we will look a little closer at a detailed list which was directed toward the knights themselves.

The knights of Europe provide a foundation of manly conduct arguably surpassed by none. The basis of this is what is referred to in our time as the *Chivalric Code* or the Code of Chivalry. It was designed to be a conduct of proper manhood, and it encompassed nearly all aspects of this to perfection.

Fear God and maintain His Church.

In the modern time it is fashionable to shun religion and spirituality. This was never the case for the knights. Religion was central to their life.

While is it not as easy to be open about such things in our time, religiosity is nothing to be ashamed of.

From religion, many people find comfort as well as a moral code that they might not otherwise find so easily.

If you are not a religious person, that is fine. But if you are, then following the Chivalric Code would involve actually *living* your faith, as opposed to merely showing up for Sunday services.

Serve the liege lord with valor and faith.

When pledging your sword to a liege lord, you were actually offering your life as well. It meant that, should the situation arise, you were to lay down your life (again we see the theme of sacrifice).

Valor and faith are essential here.

You are to serve with valor, which is brave but not reckless. And you are to serve with faith. Trust is placed in you, and you must live up to it, you must be worthy.

In our time, we no longer serve liege lords, but this does not mean we are free of commitments and obligations. If we are employed, we have obligations to our boss. If we are an employer, we have obligations to our employees. If we are married, we have obligations and responsibilities to our Wife. If we are a Father, we also have further obligations and responsibilities to our children.

Fulfilling these obligations can sometimes take valor, especially when there are temptations to do otherwise. But always, our obligations and responsibilities require that we fulfill them faithfully.

Do not fall short on this, or the regrets will be tremendous.

And a quick return to the thought on valor. We noted that valor is not reckless. This is not the act of the berserker throwing his life away in order to go out in a blaze of glory. Valor can mean negotiating peace from a position of strength. Valor is standing for what is right in spite of any personal danger. We need a lot more of that in our time. Too many people are simply seeking personal moments of fame and they do not consider whether or not what they are doing is right.

Protect the weak and defenseless.

It is a mistake of epic proportions to turn your back on the genetic obligation of being a man. Our two main purposes in life are to protect the family and to provide for them.

Protection is key. A man should be willing and able to protect those who are unable to protect themselves.

It is common in our day to make fun of the weak. There are those who opt to project an air of harmlessness, men who try to avoid offending those who are offended by anything masculine. These men choose this path, and their choice might offend our code of conduct, but this does not mean that we will stand idly by while the predator human devours them. One person is living their life, while the other is destroying another's life. Society has mandated that the modern man be harmless. There are people who will do this sensing it as an obligation to a society that deems it as the *right thing to do.*

It is almost impossible to not feel that they were attacked because they were weak, but it is entirely unacceptable to allow them to be devoured.

It is possible to disagree with the way a person chooses to live, but the fact remains that *it is their life to live.* It is not your duty to choose for them, just as it is not for the predator to destroy them.

When we choose to be strong and live by a code of honor, we take on the responsibility of protecting those weaker than we are. *Why* they are weaker is irrelevant. We have a job to do.

Protecting women comes naturally, and men will do this without being asked. Protecting children should come naturally, but it does not always seem to be the case. Protecting other men is not always instinctive, but if we are to be the protector of those in danger, then we need to take the role seriously and do what needs to be done. Fight for what is right.

We may be unappreciated, but this does not mean we are unnecessary. Do not fall for this lie told and retold by those who hate us.

Give comfort to widows and orphans.

Throughout history, men have been the primary victims of war. We were always the ones out fighting and dying, and we accepted the role of being the expendable ones.

Some men survive the conflict and get to go home. It should be the responsibility of the men who are still around after the wars are over to care for the families who were left behind.

To this end, we can donate time and money to charities that work to help the widows and orphans of fallen soldiers. They are too ones who have lost the most.

Refrain from giving offense.

It is a common theme in our time to try to share the most offensive thoughts possible to try to gain some small degree of fame.

This fame is shallow and very fleeting, but people seem to crave it without satiety. Of course, whether or not our offense is going to be considered "okay" will depend on which side of the debate our offense offends.

It is actually a complicated game, and kind of stupid.

To the superior man, all of this is petty and unnecessary. And fame is unhealthy anyway. It is better to pursue truth and a better way to live.

In our time, there is no real way to not offend *someone,* regardless of the care we take in our conduct and the thoughtful way in which we select our words.

It is without doubt that this book itself offends *someone* out there. What we are attempting in this precept is to avoid giving offense unnecessarily or intentionally. Try your best!

Live by honor, and live for glory.

You must have a code to live by honor, but once

you have a code, you must stand by it in good faith.

Without honor, a man has very little left to his name. Stick to your code, even when it is difficult or causes you inconvenience.

Living for glory in our time is different. To the knight, it meant being heroic and brave on the field of battle. For our purposes here, think of the glory of being recognized as outstanding in your field.

When you separate yourself from the rest of the pack, and show yourself to be superior, there is a great feeling in being recognized as such by your peers.

There is nothing wrong with seeking to stand out for being great at what you do. This is far different from trying to come up with a post on one social media platform or another that goes viral.

Take pride in excellence instead of being just another flash-in-the-pan social media sensation that does nothing more than cause the further dumbing down of society. We already have enough of that.

Live a life of purpose rather than the life of an attention hound.

Despise pecuniary reward.

It is the often pondered problem. We *need* money, we *have to have it*. We go to work and sacrifice family time in order to earn it.

But do you *live* for money?

A man does what must be done. Going to work is the modern version of going out to hunt for the tribe. It is how we provide for our family these days.

But this should never lead us to believe that money is our purpose.

Providing is our purpose, our Wife and children cannot eat dollar bills and expect to survive.

So for us and our purposes here, to despise the pecuniary (monetary) reward is to despise the necessity of money, not the earning.

We do not place our focus on the dollars, but on what our family does with the money we earn.

Spend it wisely.

There are those who spend money on material items for their family. There are others who spend money on experiences, like vacations instead. And the truth is that there are people in both categories who find great happiness in either of these choices. It is not for me to tell you which one will bring you greater happiness.

What I *can* tell you is that I prefer to spend money on experiences. This does have the drawback on leaving nothing to show for the money spend, except memories.

And *that* is precisely why I find it to be the better choice for me. You might see things differently than I do.

Follow what you think is best.

Fight for the welfare of all.

It is obvious that one cannot fight for the welfare of all. Whomever you are fighting against is not going to experience your generous nature toward the ephemeral *welfare of all*.

The welfare of all which is the essence of this precept is a welfare of all who are pursuing the good. Everyone may have a slightly differing definition of what is *the good*, but everyone knows the good when they see it.

At every opportunity, we should offer every support available to us to benefit others. When there is a tragedy, we can offer support to reputable charities, or offer our services when we have the requisite skills needed in such times.

Help people when you are able to do so. This is never a bad thing, and it makes you a stronger person.

Obey those placed in authority.

We are not even taught to *respect* authority in our time, much less *obey* it.

This is our great failing.

Authority exists for a reason. If people were perfect, there would be no need for authority.

Unfortunately, people are not yet perfect, and it does not appear that perfection is going to happen anytime soon. Perfection is rather elusive.

In our time, the authority we speak of here may be our boss, but it also includes Law Enforcement. We must obey the law in order to help keep our society moving in the proper direction.

Disobeying those in authority, disobeying the law, causes disharmony in society at large. When we act in such ways, we cause more harm than good.

In our time it is common to *protest* anything and everything we do not agree with. Protests do no harm when they are organized toward a specific end.

But when the end goal is unclear, and the main purpose of the protest is to resist and disrupt society, we are nothing more than a societal version of vandals, and that is absolutely pathetic.

As a man, we are supposed to be better than that. We are supposed to make our family better, and our tribe (society).

Guard the honor of fellow knights.

The Chivalric Knights had a lofty reputation. They were viewed by commoners as heroes, but also as being better than normal people. They had a reputation that preceded them, and in many cases probably *exceeded* them.

If you are really lucky, you have some men in your life that you think of as brothers. If you are so lucky, you should take care to guard their honor. If you see them doing something that will bring them shame, be the first to privately tell them what you see happening. Give them the opportunity to correct the wrong, but do so out of the public eye. Do not shame them in front of others. Give them the benefit of the doubt as well as the chance to change course.

They will thank you later.

Be not unfair, mean, or deceitful.

This boils down to treating people right. Many times, the people who are the first to scream that they are being treated unfairly, or that someone is being mean, or that they have been lied to by someone are also the very same people who treat others in this exact manner.

When you get to the basics, there is nothing magical about treating others fairly. Often we get confused in our time that we are supposed to treat everyone equally, but this is a mistaken premise.

Suppose that there is a person you see every day at work. And further suppose that every time you see him, he tries to set you on fire. He has no particular reason for this pyromaniac proclivity towards you, it is just his personal method of self-actualization, and we are taught that self-actualization *has* to be a good thing. Right?

And further imagine that there is someone else you see every day at work, and every time he sees you, he gives you bacon. Again, there is no particular reason for this pork sharing behavior, it is just the way he is.

Is it reasonable at all to think that you are supposed to treat these two people equally?

Absolutely not!

Obviously, this is an exaggerated example. But the point remains, treating everyone equally is asinine.

But treating everyone fairly is still, and will always be, entirely appropriate.

Keep the faith.

For the knight, this precept would have had a deep religious meaning. And if it has one for you, that is a great thing.

Keeping the faith for a religious person will cover much of what it means to be a good man. If this is how the precept strikes you, go with that.

For the nonreligious or the semi-religious, this precept might be met with a degree of mistrust.

This is fine.

If this category applies to you, there is another way to approach the precept that will allow you to put it into practice without the side issues.

Keeping the faith can also mean being true to your word. When you marry, you give your word to be faithful. When you Father children you are giving your word to be committed to raising them right and giving them the tools they need to be successful in life.

So keep the faith. Live up to your word and your commitments.

Always speak the truth.

Lying is easy. It is easy enough that it can be called the cowards way.

Sometimes being truthful is very difficult. There are truths which are hard to speak, and often we may fear what we will have to face if someone knows a difficult truth about us or hears it from us.

We must still tell it.

The path of lying is easy, but only at first.

We will end up needing to tell a lie to cover the lie.

And later still we will have to lie about the lie we used to cover our ass over the original lie. And so it goes on and on and on.

Honesty is always best, even when it isn't easy or fun. This seems to be a part of a running theme in this book, but maybe the truth bears repeating.

Once started, persevere to the end of any task.

A man is not supposed to be a quitter.

Quitting is for the weak, men are made to suffer and endure bitterness. We are tough in this manner.

In our time there are many men who simply take whatever pleasure they can, but then disappear when responsibility rears its head.

It is a sad fact that there are many men who participate in the undeniably enjoyable act of procreation, only to run and hide from the responsibility of raising children.

This is unconscionable.

Life is about much more than momentary pleasures, and women are more than just a couple of parts that make us crazy.

There are joys in Fatherhood that are worth more than anything else in the world, provided you are there to experience them.

This is but one example, but an entire book could be written on the fact that life is so much more than drinking and sex.

Enjoy the finer things in life, but there is great joy to be found in the traditional role filled by being a good man. Find that joy and you will live a life worth remembering.

Life is not just sensual pleasures. To think that your senses must always be stimulated with pleasure is setting yourself up for a disappointment.

Fulfill your commitments and obligations as if your entire life depended on it. The sad truth is, *someone's* life actually does depend on it. What you do has an effect on the lives of others too.

Finish what you start, and finish strong.

Respect the honor of women.

Women are to be respected, not because they are women but because they are *people*.

Many men think of women as being a life support system for a vagina, and this is worse than pathetic. It gives all men a bad name and a bad reputation.

If you are willing to have sex with a woman, be sure that you are willing to raise children with her too. Even the most trusted birth control methods fail, and life is not a card game.

Just as we want to be respected as men, and want to be recognized for what men contribute to society and the world, women want the same. They want to be recognized and appreciated for what they give to society and to the world, and they contribute a lot.

Recognizing the enormous contributions of women to the world in no way diminishes us as men, and it does not diminish the contributions of men!

Be respectful of women.

Never refuse a challenge from an equal.

This precept requires a close look. It is one thing to accept all challenges, because as your reputation grows, you will receive challenges from many people who are simply unqualified to challenge you. Beating them will bolster your confidence in a way, but it does nothing for your reputation in the eyes of people who know the game.

It becomes clear that accepting *all* challenges is nothing special.

But accepting challenges from equals is another matter entirely.

In the modern world, we do not have challenges to fights, at least outside of the martial arts world.

However, you may find that you are being challenged from a coworker, perhaps they want your position, or they want to impress the bosses.

Meet the challenges head on, do not shy away from them. You have something to lose should you fail, but you will not fail. The inexperienced tend to think that they know more than the experienced, and this is the folly of youth.

Meet the challenge head on and teach them the lessons you learned long ago.

Never turn you back on a foe.

There are people you simply have no reason to trust.

There is no good reason to let your guard down around them.

Many people are slaves to their base instincts, and cannot see past their own ambition. Let them fail.

Win through experience.

Turning your back on someone who has ill will toward you is foolish.

If you even suspect that a person wishes you harm, or wants your status, do not give them an opening to exploit. You can defeat any enemy if you see them and recognize who and what they are. But the first part of this is *seeing*.

Do not deny who or what they are, or what they

are trying to accomplish.

Notes: The knights have much to teach us about manhood.

They lived a life wherein they understood fully that it was their duty to die. With death in their face every day, they had a deeper understanding of what was important, and what was not, than we will ever have.

It is impossible to not gain this clarity when you are faced with your own mortality.

We tend to allow ourselves to think that we have forever. We brush aside any thoughts that pop into our heads that we will one day die, and we live our lives as if we have forever, but we only truly have now.

Without facing our own finite existence, we cannot hope to live fully, and we will have no hope of understanding how important this *now* is.

For as long as we allow ourselves the delusion that we are more than what we are, we will never be able to understand how precious every moment is, and how important it is to act the way we should.

We have many opportunities every day to do some good, be of service, to make the world a better place, and help people. This was a part of the knight's life mission, and we can make it a part of our own as well.

With an understanding of what is and is not important, they lived full lives, but also they also served as a great example of what is possible if we choose to be real men. Learn from them.

9 The Vikings

Category: Warrior Culture
Origin: Scandinavia

There isn't a man alive who has not heard of the Vikings, and every man has admired them at some point in his life.

There is something about this particular warrior culture that tends to resonate with young men. Perhaps it was the seafaring lifestyle, every man has had a point in his life where he was affected by wanderlust. It could also be the tremendous reputation of badassery.

Vikings were brutal fighters who offered no mercy to their enemies. Vikings kicked major ass and their influence on history is undeniable.

But to offer the Viking culture as a model of masculinity in our time will require some explanation.

Like any hero, the Vikings were viewed as terribly evil by their enemies. To themselves and among their own, they were simply doing what Vikings do.

Much like in our time when men are told that it is wrong to look at a beautiful woman, this goes against our nature. We are hardwired to notice visual beauty. In the same way, Vikings were conditioned to show no mercy to their foes, to them it was absolutely normal. This is not necessarily a nice fact, but it is a fact nonetheless.

It is too easy to sit from our technological armchair and pass judgement that the Vikings were brutal plunderers, and somehow beneath us.

The fact is that in their time the behavior of the Vikings was nothing more than normal. It is not politically correct to say, but there was a time in human history where much of what we consider as *evil* was simply the way things were done, it was the way of the world.

In placing ourselves into the proper mindset, we have an opportunity to see the Vikings as *they* viewed themselves. In this way we can see a path to adopt their code of conduct into our own lives, without the plundering, of course.

So, what was the Viking code of ethics?

Surprisingly, it was comprised of things that anyone in their right mind could support! As we shall see as this chapter progresses, when we strip away our biases, we can see the humanity of a people who were excessively violent by modern standards, but were simply doing the best that they knew how to do by their own standards.

Just as we ourselves may one day be judged by posterity as being boorish knuckleheads, we tend to forget that people of the past had a different *normal*. They were more like us than we might think. Let us take a look at the ethics of the

Vikings and just how we might apply their ethics in our own life.

Brotherhood

When discussing the Viking code, we must understand the concept of brotherhood as applied to the life of the Viking.

The Vikings were seafarers. Travel by sea was treacherous at best, and what they were up to once they reached their destination was dangerous.

Raiding, pillaging, piracy on the open sea, these are activities which do not lead to a long life. They needed to be able to count on each man beside them to guard their blind side.

In our time this brotherhood is seen a lot less often. Some boys get to learn it through sports, but often as not sports are viewed as *toxic*, and therefore shunned.

How dare we teach our boys to compete!

If you have a group of male friends who consider one another to be brothers, you have something truly special. Don't use the word brotherhood lightly, but when it is appropriate, use it, and it will be instantly recognizable to any man.

Whether you have brothers by blood and birth, or

if you have friends that you know you can count on for anything, you know what brotherhood is. Earn it, treasure it, and strive to be worthy of that brotherhood.

Loyalty

Loyalty to the Viking had a deeper meaning than it does in our time. A Viking would sacrifice his life if the sole reward was that his brothers and his family would be proud of him.

We do not take loyalty that seriously in our time, but it would be a good thing if we did. This is not to say that we should cast our lives away recklessly, but if people actually *cared* about other people...*that* would be a great start to a better place.

If men would actually consider the cost of their own disloyalty, paid for by those around them and who are dependent upon them, we'd get to a better place.

Be that person that your friends can count on. Be dependable and available. When a friend or family member needs help, be the first one there for them. If at all possible, strive to not be the first person to give up on someone. Loyalty involves placing your faith in someone. Sometimes you will regret it, but it is still worth the risk.

None of this involves giving up your rational

thinking. If a person is taking advantage of you and using your loyalty for their own benefit and at your expense, then you might need to cut them loose and get them out of your life.

Each case is different, but with time and effort you will learn to see when it is time to stay, or go.

Honor

In the Viking age, your word was an oath. It had to be kept regardless of the cost. In Viking culture, your word was a legal obligation. The obligation carried a great responsibility to the man because it was not just his own reputation at risk, it was the reputation of his entire family.

We do not often consider what happens to those around us when we break our word. In our time it is common to act as if we are cool because people were duped into trusting us.

The people who act in this way are worse than stupid, they are ignorant[9]. Everything in every culture screams that we must value honor, and yet...here we are. Trying to teach our youth that doing the right thing is the best path.

Honor is not a quaint thing of the past. It is simply

---

[9] Stupid people just don't know any better. Ignorant people actually know better than to do stupid things, they just opt to do the stupid things anyway.

overshadowed in our time by the wish for fame. In the end, you will regret sacrificing your honor more than you could ever regret missing out on fame.

Guard your honor, follow through on your promises, everything that has been repeated throughout this book has a message. The warrior cultures are screaming to us that *these things matter*!

Courage

To the Viking, it was the fool who sought peace through avoiding conflict. Conflict is a part of life, even in our modern time, much more so in the age of the Vikings.

Those who are brave live a life with fewer regrets and less sorrow. The brave live the full life.

In our time, the way of the coward is prized. Men are not only taught that conflict is to be avoided, but that competition is bad. True enough, in our time, there are legal hassles if conflict goes too far. But there are failure issues if trying to avoid all conflict goes too far.

A man should never become a complete doormat in an effort to be non-confrontational. You have to stand up for what is right, and sometimes what is right is going to need to be demanded. This is because there are people who will take advantage of the person who will not stand up. Sometimes a man has to stand up and stare down wrongdoing and mistreatment of himself or others.

Courage is often learned through the childhood games of boys. When competing in sports like wrestling, the boys learn to keep struggling even when they are in pain and even when defeat is imminent.

Without such lessons, we end up with men who need spaces to go and cry if someone says mean things to them.

No coach in any sport expects every boy to become a world class athlete. But every boy should experience good coaching, and good coaching involves heavy doses of being told that you are doing a terrible job every time that you are not giving 100%. It does the boy good.

Respect

To the Viking, respect must begin with self-respect. If you respect yourself, then you will take care of your reputation first, because your reputation affects your entire family.

Once this is a standard form of behavior, then you can begin the arduous process of *earning* the respect of others. You could only earn the respect of others in the Viking society if you did not dishonor yourself and your family.

It is easy in our time to demand that people respect you even when you have done nothing whatsoever to earn it. You will not truly gain respect in this way, but you might bully some people into faking it to your face.

However, earning the respect of others is always worth the effort. Respect yourself, and respect others, in this way others will have a reason to respect you as well.

Strength

Strength was prized to one degree or another in all warrior cultures. To the Vikings, it was highly prized.

The life of the Norseman was hard. The weather, the travel, the wars, none of this was for the weak.

The weak died, but the strong survived.

In our time, we find many groups that are vehemently opposed to the traditionally strong male. We are told that strength in a man is a method of oppressing women, when this is not now, and never has been the case.

Men had to be strong in the traditional cultures in order to protect family and tribe. Rather than accept the shame that is pressed upon us without just cause, men should simply do what men have always done; develop the strength necessary to protect our loved ones.

Do not be afraid of what you might hear from the whiny and overly protesting youth of our time.

Be strong physically and mentally. You will need both types of strength in this world, develop them to the best of your ability.

You do not have to become a bodybuilder or a pro athlete, but get as strong as you can. It helps.

Perseverance

In the age of the Vikings, perseverance, pressing ahead regardless of personal hardship, was another quality that was revered. Within their culture, even if a man had been wounded or even mutilated, he was valued by clan and family if he kept moving forward. A man could not be considered useless if he still pressed on and proved through his own effort that he would not be denied.

In our time, we could do well to learn this lesson. How often do we see what is really nothing more than a setback as a complete defeat? This is the exact opposite of perseverance. Setbacks and challenges are just setbacks and challenges, not the end of the world or even a final estimate of our personal worth.

Learn to press on and not accept defeat. This

perseverance will start to set you apart from the crowd.

Discipline

The lazy are not victorious. Discipline is the key to defeating laziness. When a person is disciplined they act *deliberately*. The disciplined man is in control of, and not controlled by his impulses.

We often mistake the idea of discipline as being the ability to sit still, but this is far from the truth. A lazy person is quite capable of sitting still all day, but this is no indication that they are disciplined.

Discipline is deliberate action, and doing what needs to be done simply because it needs to be done.

To the Viking there was too much on the line to allow for laziness. Lives could be lost from such traits, and it could be your own life lost, or that of a brother, and in either case, lives lost due to laziness were completely avoidable and thus unacceptable.

Discipline yourself to face whatever you need to face, and choose your actions and responses wisely.

Self-reliance

To the Viking, it was a shame to himself and his family to be a burden. To prevent this, the Viking developed a finely tuned self-reliance, never counting on others to do for him what he could or should do for himself.

It is too easy in our day to allow others to do for us what we should do for ourselves. Whether those others are the custodial staff or some nameless, faceless bureaucrat in some government office.

Anything that you can do for yourself, do.

Self-reliance was, at one time, the most American trait we could name. The *gimme gimme gimme* mentality of our time is the antithesis of what we, as a nation, once were. Politicians in our day are elected based on what freebies they offer to the voting public. Given the choice between being free and letting the government take care of us, most voters in our time want the later.

A man who takes pride in himself will always choose to be self-reliant. Personally, I take great pride in the fact that I never ask anyone for anything. If there is something I need, I get it. If there is something that needs to be done, I do it.

Self-reliance is really hardwired into the brain of a man.

Justice

The age of glory for the Vikings was a long time ago. But when you take a society comprised of very strong men who were quite capable of violent actions, those in charge of governing needed to be just in their rulings or the people would simply take matters into their own hands.

Gone are the days when an injustice would result in a generations-long blood feud. Thankfully, such things are of the past.

But justice is still important. We are not speaking here of the ephemeral *social justice* of the modern day. Such causes are intentionally unfulfillable (and that is why they are so vaguely defined). To the modern man, a sense of justice can be related to the sporting concept of *fair play*. Playing by the rules is not always the easy choice, but we can include it in our idea of justice because it cannot come back to bite us if we treat people fairly.

Notes: To the Viking in his time, what a Viking did was simply what a man was *supposed* to do. If you were to ask a Viking what he did, he would likely respond that he was a farmer. He did not identify as a warrior or any other such notion. He was who he was back at home. When he had to go on these campaigns, he was simply doing what had to be done as a man.

It is quite possible in our day to adopt the Viking code as your own. Every man has things in his life that must be done, even when they are not necessarily confined to what his job is. You can adopt this code as a means of keeping to your path, if it fits your life and goals.

Although the society that the Vikings lived in was very different from our own, there is still much to learn from them, especially in the area of masculinity.

While living by the Viking code in our time would be challenging in some aspects, there is nothing in this code that would bring you dishonor. There are values here that, while interpreted differently by different warrior cultures, were nevertheless a part of the other warrior cultures. This is a very noble set of values.

10 Hwa Rang

Category: Warrior Culture
Origin: Korea

The *Hwa Rang* were a society made up of the sons of Korean (Silla dynasty) aristocracy. Although often referred to as the "Flower Knights", this is very incorrect. The most common translation into English is the *Flowering Manhood*. It was from this group of young men that the empire would be able to identify and place the best and brightest of the nation's elite. Martial arts, dancing, singing, religious education and political indoctrination were all a part of the training of the Hwa Rang youth.

The purpose of the Hwa Rang training was to create broad-based knowledge in the men who would one day be the leaders of the nation.

As one might imagine, the sources for information about the Hwa Rang are limited. Who they were and what they believed is important for our purposes here, and we can learn a lot through looking at the virtues they chose to focus their lives on. These values were influenced by Buddhism, Taoism, Confucianism, and to some extend native Korean nature magic beliefs. They are often viewed as being a military training school or group, but they were about more than that. While there was extensive training in military arts, the true purpose of the group was to create strong men.

The skills taught to the young men in the Hwa

Rang were the skills necessary for success. Through participation in this elite group, the young men were trained in military, religion, morality, art, music, and traditional Korean values.

Because of the range of influences and the vast array of study, it is necessary to go beyond a first glance in our attempt to see if the values of the Hwa Rang can make us better men in the modern age.

사군이충: *Sa Kun E Choong* (Loyalty to Country)

In any successful nation, there has to be a sense of patriotism. Without a sense of pride in the country, the people will be troublesome. All political leaders know this. Those less scrupulous will exploit this fact, while those with a moral compass will use this knowledge to guide their own decisions.

If you have a sense of patriotism, this is a good thing. In our time, patriotism is viewed as a great thing unless you are from America. If you are from America, then you are taught to be ashamed of your country, and this is a big part of what has gone wrong in this nation.

In order to stay apolitical...

For the purposes we have here, we need to take this knowledge and use it wisely and with the purpose of making everyone around us more successful.

We all have a varying degree of leadership wherever we work. We need to find and share a sense of pride in where we work and what we do. In this way we will help those we work with to be happier. A happy employee is a productive employee. When we can make those we are in charge of happier and more productive, we will become noticed as a leader of men.

Patriotism is really loyalty to Country, and as a virtue, loyalty is an indispensable character strength.

사친이효: Sa Chin E (Filial Piety)

Whenever possible, it is the duty of the child to care for the parents as they age. Bad blood can develop, but a son must remember that the parents took care of him when he was incapable of taking care of himself. There is a debt involved in this, and this debt cannot be overlooked or swept under the rug.

If things go well for you in your life, you will one day be old as well. And you will need help with things that were once easy for you. This is a perpetual circle.

Again we see the theme of a man fulfilling his responsibilities, even when they are challenging or difficult to fulfill.

While your parents live, it is a good thing for you to help to make sure that they have everything they need. You will miss them when they are gone.

교우이신: Kyo Woo E Shin (Trust your Brothers)

In battle, you have to trust the people around you. If there is any weakness in your group, there will be a slaughter. Training together develops this trust. You learn the strengths and weaknesses of your brothers in arms, and those in charge are able to set plans accordingly.

In our day, there is often a lot of mistrust by men, especially when it comes to other men. This must be overcome as it is a character weakness. It is a sign that the constant barrage of accusations against anything and everything masculine is starting to sink in and poison your mind. Give your brothers the benefit of the doubt, or at least give them a chance to fail. If they do, fail cut them out of your life, but if they prove out, count them among your family.

임전무퇴: Im Jeon Moo Tae (Courage, never retreat)

On the battlefield, it may be wise at certain times to retreat, or to give the impression of retreating, but this is not how winning is done. The courageous may fall in battle, but they also may cause the enemy to run.

In our day, men are so beaten down and under constant attack that it might seem worth it to run from the fight. We may want to back down to avoid all conflict. But we are the people our sons are looking to for guidance.

Men are supposed to be men. Sometimes we have to face those who are wrong and tell them that they are wrong. This takes courage, and a willingness to stand your ground.

살생유택: Sal Saeng Yoo Teak (Always make a just kill)

Indiscriminate killing is frowned upon by all civilized societies. This is a given. There have been a few warrior societies wherein the killing of people in the lower classes, or more often killing condemned criminals, was allowed and even celebrated. But by and large, wanton killing was considered to be beneath the warrior. This is probably based on a much older tradition, dating back to when the warrior, the male's role in the society boiled down to providing food and protecting the tribe, and randomly killing members of the tribe only served to make the tribe smaller, and thus, more vulnerable to attack from other tribes.

Of course, in our society today, we are taught that *all* violence is bad. This reasoning is the basis for most of the attacks on masculinity. But those who make such attacks ignore the necessity of strong men to protect the weaker people within their own society. While a man should never be sitting around waiting for an opportunity to kill someone, we should be trained and capable of stopping the threat from those people who prey on the weak. But we also need to have the wisdom to know when to stop.

To use an example from the news. There was an attack in a workplace. There happened to be a person on-site who was legally carrying a concealed firearm. Security footage shows the hero draw his weapon, order the attacker to stop, and once the attacker was noncompliant, the hero fired one shot which dropped the attacker to the ground and caused him to lose his weapon. At this point the hero moves closer, kicks the bad guy's weapon out of reach, and then he *holsters his own weapon*, because the threat was no longer a threat.

The macho, Hollywood type of nonsense might have been to put a few more rounds into the bad guy to "finish the job", but this would have not only been illegal, it would have been immoral. The only reason our good guy had for drawing his weapon was to stop the bad guy from shooting innocent people. Once this task is complete, there is no need for the weapon to be out. We must remember that we *might* need to kill, but we will not *always* need to kill, and we should always use the minimum force necessary to stop the threat. Then we are living up to this ideal of the Hwa Rang.

Notes: The Hwa Rang youth group was exclusively male. This would, of course, be frowned upon in our society, and they would either be forced to bring in female members, or else it would simply be broadcasted as a misogynist group, and publicly shamed until it closed up shop for good.

This is a shame, because young men do need some time to just be around other young men under the guidance of an adult man. It is chastised as sexist to say this, but it is no different from young women needing to be around older women who will guide them.

The core values of the Hwa Rang were of a high order. This was a powerfully focused group that was intended to guide the young aristocracy. This was done quite well, as we can see from the preceding list.

The ideas of patriotism, keeping to the family, only doing what is right – these are great ideals to live by. And they will take you far beyond the mere living of a life by random happenstance. When setting your code of conduct, it is best to set the bar high. There is nothing great to be achieved in living by a code that is set at the bare minimum that you already think you are capable of doing, push yourself to be the best that you can be!

One could do much worse than to use the values espoused by the Hwa Rang as the core of their own code of manhood.

11 The Filipino Warriors

Category: Warrior Culture
Origin: the Philippines

There are certain warrior cultures and martial traditions that command respect, and which are held in high regard even by people who are not of their lineage and do not practice their style or system. The martial arts of the Philippines are in this category. With stick and blade, the Filipino arts are without peer, and with empty hands they are still extremely formidable.

The martial arts of the Philippines are well known for a variety of skills; empty-hand, blunt-force weapons, edged weapons, and even grappling skills are a part of the traditional Filipino martial arts. Add to this mix the extensive training on being able to transition from any of these skill sets into another and one can begin to see the reason for the respect given by the martial arts community to the Filipino systems.

Given the straight-forward emphasis on realism, the Filipino martial arts reply heavily on weapons training. Whether we like to admit it or not, weapons are an equalizer in fights. Most women would lose in a fist fight against a large man, but give the woman a gun, and the playing field is suddenly level.

Although the Philippines was a colony of Spain, and America, and was brutalized by the Japanese, some areas were never really conquered in the truest sense of the word.

The Moros in the south and the Ifugao, Bontoc, Ilonggot, Sagada, Igorot, and the Isnag of Kalinga Apayao of the north were a thorn in the side of those who would rule over them, and some still cause troubles to this day. They were also fighters like you wouldn't believe. Even in areas which were colonized, we can see simple farm tools were also turned into great weapons, such as the bolo knife and the karambit[10].

Additionally, the Filipino martial arts teach that these traditional weapons are still practical today, and how to use these traditional weapons against

---

[10] The Karambit is enjoying a degree of popularity among the prepper crowd. It is really designed for gutting pigs and is truly a farm tool.

the modern weapons one might be faced with against the modern armed criminal.

But the Filipino martial arts also contain a traditional code of ethics that make their warrior culture something that can be used by the modern man, just as much as he can use a traditional weapon in the modern time. The Filipino martial culture is as ethical as it is deadly. Hence, it is contained in this book.

Integredad (Integrity)

Part of the running theme of the warrior cultures is a stress placed upon the importance of integrity. Men abhor liars. Dishonesty is not only viewed with contempt, it is dangerous to the whole. You deceive yourself and those around you, and in the warrior culture, this can cause your own death and the deaths of those around you.

A lack of integrity should be frowned upon because there is still a high value placed upon trust. If a person is trustworthy, they are raised up, but if they are not, they are attacked without mercy.

In the age of *trial by twitter*, mere accusations are enough to ruin a personal reputation. As has been taught for a long time, honesty is still the best policy.

As has been said repeatedly, you won't be wrong by doing right.

Disiplina (Discipline)

Within the warrior cultures, the man must have discipline, his actions must be intentional, chosen, directed by his own will.

To a warrior, impulsive action is reckless because it is based on emotions, and emotion based decisions usually end in disaster.

In our day, it is easy to see what happens to people who let their emotions control their actions. They end up losing their job over a social media tirade, or they end up in a physical fight over a difference of political opinion. Such stupidity is best reserved for teenagers. A man has to keep his wits and his reason active at all times to avoid looking like a fool or a child.

Be a man of discipline. Act intentionally, and do not let emotion rule your decision making process. Mistakes come easy when you are in an emotional state. It takes discipline to not fall into the trap of emotion based decisions, so practice discipline at every moment.

Start small if you have to. When the alarm goes off, get your ass out of bed immediately. If you have a deadline at work, meet it or beat it.

Remember, we were built for more hardship than we face in our time. Men of discipline will thrive.

Responsibilidad (Responsibility)

In a warrior culture, the man owns his actions. He will accept the glory or the responsibility for what he has done, and in neither case will he be heard complaining.

While responsibility is often discussed by the modern man, it is much more rarely put into practice.

Just look at the alarming number of children who are growing up without a Father in their lives, and consider the impact his is having on our society as a whole.

The number of men who simply walk away from their role as a Father is staggering, and is as true a condemnation of the men of our age as one is likely to find.

Whether you create a child or sign a contract, you are pledging your name to fulfill your obligations. Be a man and take care of business. Do what has to be done. In the end, you will be a better man for it, and those around you will think more highly of you.

When you were a child, you had no real

responsibilities. But as you grow up, this changes. Everyone had it easier as a child, but a man cannot be a child. Be a man and handle your responsibilities like a real man.

Pagkamasunurin (Obedience)

Within the martial arts there is a common theme of obedience to the instructor. This is a hard task for most modern people, and on the surface it might seem to run counter to any code of manliness. But martial arts are typically based on warrior cultures, and thus, military in nature. Being military in nature, we can see the importance and value of obedience as a virtue among men.

If you are not a martial artist or soldier, there is still a place in the life of a man to value obedience. For a start, one must obey the law. This is essential for both freedom and a long and healthy life.

One must also obey their code of ethics, whatever yours may be. Having a code is easy, living by a code takes work, and it takes obedience to the rules you have chosen to live by. As the old saying goes, if it were easy, everyone would do it.

As an employee, you must follow company rules and guidelines. Again, this takes obedience.

Obedience does not mean that you become a

doormat for anyone. This is counterproductive to living fully as a man. There is nothing wrong with demanding that others treat you in the same manner that you treat them. You do not have to be a jerk about it, but you can insist on being treated fairly.

Kapakumbabaan (Humility)

Again we see a culture wherein there is a prized value of humility.

Those people who are selfish are easily contemptable. There is no real value in those people, and this is part of why they are despised universally.

Taking things a step further, those who are humble are also those who are lifelong learners. They do not sit back on their accomplishments and talk about how great they used to be. Instead, they seek out new challenges and new tasks to bring them to deeper knowledge or greater understanding.

No matter how much you know or how good you are, there will always be someone who knows more or who is better than you in your chosen field. Keeping this thought in the front of your mind will drive you to seek constant improvement, and this is a goal worthy of anyone wishing to be the best man that they can be.

Do not allow yourself to fall into the trap of thinking that you know more than anyone else. It is well and good to believe in yourself and recognize that you have talents and skills, but you do not want to become one of those people who feel the need to be worshiped. No one likes those people. Be better.

Kawanggawa (Charity)

Charity might seem like a strange quality for a warrior to prize. Look closer. There is, universally, no pride in taking a life wantonly. Discipline is required if you are to stop the fight when the threat is no longer a threat. Charity will be the driving force behind this for the warrior. Mercy is a charity.

And charity is helping others because you can.

A person living by a warrior code of ethics is going to help a person because they can, whether this means helping to change a tire on the side of the road or defending a person from a mugging.

There are many ways in which a man can help people in our modern society. Donate you time to a nonprofit of your choice. Donate money if you are able to do so. There is bound to be a cause that means something to you. Take steps to actually be a benefit to that cause, through your time, labor, or money.

Everyone has a cause they feel deeply about, but most people in our time think that talking about an issue on social media is "doing something", or even more pathetically, "helping".

It isn't doing either. Social media post are not helping. Helping is helping. If you want to help, volunteer your time and be productive.

Pagkamakabayan (Patriotism)

There is no warrior culture on earth that does not prize or otherwise seek to instill a sense of patriotism within the hearts and minds of their soldiers. There are many reasons for this. For a start, if you do not love your country, you should either work to change your country, or leave it for the one you prefer, if a better one exists in your mind.

But at the heart of patriotism is a love of something greater than yourself. If all you can manage is to find fault and reasons to hate, you are going to be a poor human being.

It is a higher level of thinking that allows you to find reasons to appreciate what you have and where you live.

Further, if you have the ability to love your country, you will be willing to fight for it. Just as if you love your family or your wife or your children, you will fight for them and defend and protect them. Duty to country is an ancient concept as it started with love of tribe, and for most of us, the modern tribe is our family.

If you can find a sense of patriotism, you will be able to see your family as a microcosm of that feeling. It will not take much from that point to see the value to be places on this ethic.

Notes: As a Nation, the Philippines has been colonized by different nations throughout her history, but through it all she has maintained a sense of self.

The modern man can learn from this. Being true to yourself and who you really are is a sign of great internal strength, especially when you can be true to who you are in spite of external pressures to be different from what you are.

As for these values, while many are shared by other warrior cultures, they are taken to heart by the Filipinos in a unique way. Filipinos are Asian, but European. They are Eastern and Western, and they do not apologize for this, they embrace it.

They are the only Catholic nation in Asia. Again,

they do not hide or make excuses for this, it is just a part of who they are.

As warriors, they are on par with any other nation on earth. As a people they are among the finest I have ever had the pleasure to be around. They live their values openly. We could all do well to learn from them, even if we only learn to live out our professed values.

Beyond this, we can look to the values themselves, a code of conduct for men that is without flaw. Anyone can adopt this code as their own and they would live a life to be admired.

The two values that stand out the most to me are obedience and charity.

For me, obedience would be the obedience to the code of conduct. Having a code is meaningless if you do not follow it. This is a stress on the importance of *actually* living by what you profess.

The inclusion of charity is also very important. This is about helping others. It is easy to become overly focused on self-improvement and reach the point where you do not even consider the welfare of others. But how good are you as a human being or as a man, really, if you are not doing good for others?

Not very good at all, honestly.

So this reaches a point where we see that, while it is important to work on the self, and the improvement of our own conduct and ability to live by our code, it is equally important to be able and willing to help others so that they too can be the best that they can be. If we are not doing something for those beyond ourselves, how is it that we can ever expect our lives to mean anything beyond our own moment?

A man has to consider his legacy. What about us lives on after we are gone?

12 Bushido

Category: Warrior Culture
Origin: Japan

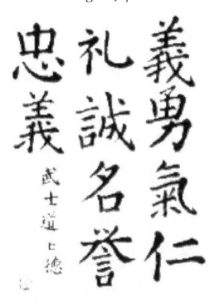

While the Samurai may or may not deserve the deification that they commonly receive in both martial art and warrior culture groups, the fact is that they were warriors of a high order. They ruled Japan and oversaw a very prosperous and gloried age.

Like any warrior culture, there is an effort placed on finding the most perfectly cultivated man to fulfill the role as warrior. It is easy to assume that these ideals are beyond our grasp, but this is unnecessarily self-limiting. Men of today are every bit as capable as the men of any other age, if only we are willing to apply ourselves and *learn*.

We find the first use of the word *Bushido* in the Edo period of Japanese history.

Bushido is usually translated as the *way of the warrior*. Volumes could be written on the topic of Bushido, but here we will focus on the *Eight Virtues*.

義 *gi* (Righteousness)

The righteousness we are looking at in this virtue is within. We are to consider our own correct action and proper motivations. This is not done with the thought of pressing our ideals on others.

Remember, living by a code is a deeply personal act. If others choose to live by your code, it is of their free will and your only part in their decision is from being a *living example*.

Do what is right, because it is the right thing to do, not because it will impress others or give you an opportunity to show others how much better than them you are.

Righteousness here is about making sure that your own conduct is correct, every action is intentional and well-reasoned, and our motivation is to be the best that we can be.

勇 yū (Courage)

True courage, the courage of a warrior, is going to be intentional action which is taken in spite of fear.

Any fool can rush headlong into the spray of gunfire - that is not courage, it is idiocy. It is casting aside life for no reason.

There is a reason why 18 year-olds are accepted into the military, they don't know they are mortal and will do absurd things like rush the enemy even if they are outnumbered. This is good when reckless abandon is needed. Those warriors who live past this stage are formidable indeed, because they have experience to anticipate and adapt to danger. Strength, intelligence, and experience create a type of courage that can accomplish great things.

In our time, courage is not always going to be in a life or death situation. As men, we are charged with bring the protectors, but some people need to start from where they are. For some people, a starting point of courage is going to be volunteering for a difficult project at work. For others it may involve taking up training in a martial art or in firearms.

Start where you are. There is no one-size-fits-all plan that can be given here to suddenly turn every man into a living example of courage. You have a bubble of security around you, but it is limiting. Be more.

仁 *jin* (Compassion)

While it is not a common thing to associate Samurai with compassion, but it is a warrior ethic that is cross cultural. And we must not forget that it is compassion, the caring for the well-being of others that drives the warrior to a point where he is willing to sacrifice his very life for those he is sworn to protect.

As modern men, we may not often be called upon to sacrifice our lives for the village, but we can still make sacrifices for those we love and commit our lives to. We should make such sacrifices willingly and without complaint. Men are built to carry the heavy load for a long distance. Carry it with a calm and uncomplaining endurance.

Respect that everyone has their own troubles. Compassion involves understanding that your problems are your own, and that to another person, your troubles seem small compared to their own.

In this perspective, we can see that when a person

is concerned with their own problems, it is because those problems are the bigger problem from their point of view.

Give them the room they need to go through what they are dealing with and help them if you can. At the very least, be a friend to them.

礼 *rei* (Respect)

Respect is, without a doubt, a universal warrior ideal. Respect can keep you safe in environments that are well outside of your known area. Respect shown to others can turn into respect given to you.

It is important to show respect to superiors, this is a duty and for most men it happens with very little thought. Respect to equals is rarer still, but is an outward manifestation of an ideal that needs to be lived. The rarest of all is the respect shown to those who can do nothing for you. This is a sign of nobility, of a truly great man.

We can put this ideal into good practice by starting at home. We should respect our wife and our children. We should take care of them and provide for our family.

We should respect ourselves enough to care about the legacy we leave behind in this world when we are gone. Like a rock cast into a pond creates ripples, our every action creates echoes that continue to change the world, for better or worse, long after we are dead and gone.

There is simply no good reason to be disrespectful at all. The times can be crude, but there is no rule that says we must be as well. Rise above and take no part in what is beneath a man.

誠 *makoto* (Honesty)

Honesty with all is an ideal which is difficult to put into action. But we must try. For the warrior, because his word was his pledge to defend home and hearth, honesty was indispensable. It is, for the Samurai as for so many other warrior cultures, a stark necessity.

Live in such a way that others can see that your word means something. We are often told in this time that words are just air. But they are not. Words carry depth and meaning and our words can influence the decisions and actions of others.

We cannot take this lightly.

If we can keep in mind how much our honest words can help other people to make better choices we can start to be a better person, a better provider, and a better leader. Stand by your word as if everything in your world depended on it. Be honest and truthful without worry as to personal cost.

How often is a man in our day called upon to stand by his word when there is no repercussion for not doing so? And if we look around with an honest eye, how many men follow through? Few enough to give a bad name to all men. Break the mold or flip the script, or whatever the hell you want to call it. Be different, be a real man. And this brings us to…

名誉 *meiyo* (Honor)

In the story of the 47 *Ronin* (masterless Samurai) we get a glimpse of the depth of the Samurai idea of Honor.

The 47 Ronin were in the service of a Samurai who was framed and forced to commit *seppuku* (ritual suicide). Instead of following custom which mandated that they follow their master in death, they became Ronin, outcasts of society. They each played their role to the hilt, seemingly becoming drunks, gamblers, and whoremongers. After a year of this ruse, they had lulled their enemy into complacency, and exacted revenge on the one who had betrayed their master. This was the depth of Samurai honor.

Honor is taking things to the next level. When you stand by your word and actually live by your code, you are acting with honor. What you say and what you do are a reflection of who you really are inside. If what you say and what you actually do are not in harmony, your honor is called into question.

It is important to a man to be taken seriously. If this is to happen, we must be true to our word and to our code. When we make a commitment, we keep it. When we make a promise, we follow through.

Stand out from the rest by doing what is right.

忠義 *chūgi* (Loyalty)

To the Samurai, loyalty was an essential and it was life or death. If they proved disloyal it meant death.

In our time, things are a little less strict, but this does not lessen the importance of loyalty. In the end of the story of the 47 Ronin, after revenge was complete, they all committed seppuku and finally followed their master into death. Honor demanded they feign dishonor in order to avenge him, loyalty demanded they follow him in death. They fulfilled both.

A man who is loyal is rare in our time. It is a great thing to set yourself apart in this way. If you care about someone other than yourself, then loyalty is easy. This, of course, runs counter to everything the modern man is described as being, but we cannot concern ourselves with the incessant ramblings of the feeble minds of weak people. Ignore what they say, and be who you are born to be.

If you are looking for a place to start, begin with what comes most naturally to a man, loyalty to family. We all have a drive to provide. I think that the men who run from commitment to family are really scared to face the consequences of failing in front of their family, and it is easier to fail out of sight. They would better serve all if they could simply face their responsibilities and do their best.

自制 *jisei* (Self-control)

A warrior who has no self-control is not a warrior, but is instead just a murderer. The warrior of old fought for causes and sacrificed his own life to protect his family and his homeland.

Killing carries a very high psychological price, but generation after generation has paid this price to protect those they love. The taking of a life is not to be done without cause and full understanding of the cost.

In our time, self-control has been brought to so base a level that people think that self-control is a child who can sit still, and if he or she cannot, then we need to drug them into stillness.

As we have stated time and time again, self-control is *deliberate action*, as opposed to impulsive action. You might *want* to stay home from work and play video games all day, but you *need* to pay your bills, and so you will (hopefully) get your ass out of bed and go to work.

A man who possesses self-control is reliable to those who depend on him, and he is formidable to those who oppose him.

Notes: It is easy to sit back in our day and age, stroke our beards, click our tongues, and lament on the savage brutes that the Samurai were. But when considered within the context of the day and age in which they lived, they were an amazing example of power and manhood. They were the apex warriors of their time.

Like other warrior cultures, there was an acceptance of death within Samurai culture, and this has been passed down to us in the codes of Bushido. When a person clearly understands that they will die, and that no amount of pretending or ignoring will change this, there is an undeniable influence on behavior and attitude. You begin to cherish time and people in a way that you did not before. You start to see that the small things really are small things and they do not require the amount of attention we typically give them. When a person reaches this level of understanding, the values listed in this chapter make perfect sense, and even more so when we think about them coming out of a warrior culture.

13 Marcus Aurelius

Category: General Badass (and Emperor!)
Origin: Rome

Marcus Aurelius was an amazing badass, and there is no doubt that he was what we would refer to in our time as a "man's man". His writings, which come to us today as the *Meditations* are a picture of what is possible if one chooses to live the values of Stoicism. He was the last Emperor of the Roman age known as the *Pax Romana*, and time of relative peace, and amazing prosperity.

Much of this chapter comes from the writings of Marcus Aurelius and a book titled *Meditations*. Meditations is a title given by later people as the writings themselves have no official title, and the writing was really intended for no one but the author.

One fascinating aspect of the Meditations is the way in which it brings the reader to look at their own biases and judgements in their own actions and the actions of others.

This section will be a little different from the other sections. I have chosen some quotes from the work of Marcus Aurelius that apply directly to the role on man. He simply wrote too much that was profound for it to be boiled down to a list of values. It is my sincere hope that this section serves as a good closing argument on being a good man and what the role of a man is in society.

The more we value things outside our control, the less control we have.

It is easy to look around and see examples of people who show very clear symptoms of mental illness over things that are not within their control, and even more so over the remedies they seek to apply to these issues they cannot control.

Beyond voting, you have no real control over politics in your country, and even less control over the political opinions of your friends and neighbors.

Since these are not under your control, why waste a ghost of a thought on them?

This is but one example but it seems to be a good point of departure for thoughts on this idea. How many other areas of your life could be improved through the practice of this ideal?

When you place your focus on things beyond your control, your stress is pointless.

The best answer to anger is silence.

Marcus Aurelius was a practitioner of a philosophy called stoicism. If you are unfamiliar with stoicism, shame on you.

At its base, stoicism is about self-control. Emotions can pull a man far off course and make him fail in his attempts to reach his goals.

Emotions are unavoidable, but we do not have to be cast about by every whim that emotion brings to us.

Sometimes we need to keep our mouths shut in order to avoid making a bad day worse. Not every thought needs to be spoken.

As a man, there are times when you must speak up. But as anger is an emotional response to something, speaking up in anger might best be delayed. You could end up saying or doing something that causes you to lose your job, or your family. Hit the pause button, and take a moment to breathe.

Today I escaped anxiety. Or no, I discarded it, because it was within me, in my own perceptions – not outside.

Anxiousness is a fear of something which has no reality except within our mind. Learn to recognize when you are creating fear out of nothing at all.

Our minds are capable of creating complex pseudo-realities, and they do this so well that sometimes we do not even know that it isn't real.

Be careful. It is far too easy to turn minor issues into monsters that have us trembling in fear. All anxiety is created in your mind. Do not overlook this fact.

As a man, you will need to face things head on, and not allow yourself to be distracted by false reasons to be anxious. Just do what needs to be done, and see things as they are and as they come.

How ridiculous and how strange to be surprised at anything which happens in life.

This is not at all unrelated to one of Musashi's precepts from the Dokkodo.

It is an important skill, to be able to see things as they truly are, without imposing our judgements and evaluations upon them.

Living without seeing things as they are is what leads people to be caught unawares.

If we can allow ourselves to see the truth, exactly as it is right now, we will see also how silly it is to see it any other way.

You're subject to sorrow, fear, jealousy, anger and inconsistency. That's the real reason you should admit that you are not wise.

Being prone to all human frailties, it is important to admit to yourself that you do not have all of the answers.

Thinking that you are any more wise, or special, or talented, or gifted than others is a fool's trap. It doesn't take a lot to be better than that.

Always keep in mind that you are a student of life, and will remain so until the end of your life, and then you can avoid missing some of the very important lessons along the way.

And for so long as you remain subject to sorrow,

fear, jealousy, anger, and inconsistency, remind yourself that you still have more to learn, and that you are not better than anyone else.

Almost nothing material is needed for a happy life, for he who has understood existence.

In the big picture, what is really more important, the kind of car you drive, or your relationship with your wife and children?

Possessions are only good for those who care most about how they are viewed by others.

For men of substance, the concern is for doing the right thing. This is where the *real* happiness is going to be found. And it is a happiness that lasts.

Somewhere in this big world there is someone who is very happy, and they have less than you have. The essential difference being that they *appreciate* what they have.

Learn to appreciate the good things in life that are not things. People tend to only notice how good it is to be healthy when they are sick, and this is a shame. Notice what is good while it is good.

Receive wealth or prosperity without arrogance; and be ready to let it go.

Life is filled with fortune and misfortune, feast

and famine. It is essential to be able to take the good *and* the bad.

Your life will go well, except when it doesn't. Strive to be even tempered in either event.

Of course, the ultimate "letting go" refers to death. Be the man who is gracious in victory and prosperity. Do the most good that you can do with what you have. But do not fall into the trap of thinking that you *deserve* to be spared the fact of death.

Death closes every life. But this does not mean that we cannot do something noble and worthwhile in our time here.

Stand up, stand apart, and be the one who actually makes a difference in the lives of those you come into contact with.

A man when he has done a good act, does not call out for others to come and see, but he goes on to another act, as a vine goes on to produce again the grapes in season.

It does not matter who gets the credit for a good deed, what matters is the deed itself. You are a man, not a monkey who receives a treat for a trick done correctly.

Focus on doing what needs to be done and avoid

wasting time and energy thinking about people knowing it was you who did the work.

I once worked in a place once where I offered an idea to the management that would be a big change, but also be a great benefit to those we worked with. The people who heard the idea took the idea and implemented it, and claimed it as their own idea.

But the idea had such a tremendous impact on what we were all doing that I never told the powers that be that it was my idea. The idea was used and the benefit was realized, and *that* is what mattered.

Sometimes the credit is not what is important, and sometimes it is okay to not be recognized for things.

Doing what needs to be done is often far more important than having people pat you on the back and tell you that you did something good.

Is any man afraid of change? What can take place without change? What then is more pleasing or more suitable to the universal nature? And can you take a hot bath unless the wood for the fire undergoes a change? And can you be nourished unless the food undergoes a change? And can anything else that is useful be accomplished without change? Do you not see then that for yourself also to change is just the same, and equally necessary for the universal nature?

Throughout your life, things will change, circumstances will change, friends will change, and even you will change. You cannot stop it and you cannot hide from it.

Every event in your life has changed you. And while it is common to say that something has changed you forever, the truth is that everything that changes you has changed you forever.

I never imagined for a moment that I would be alive when my son would no longer be. I am forever changed by that tragedy. This is a drastic change. There are also minor changes, but even minor changes are still changes.

As your life progresses things will change.

But Billy doesn't like change.

Well, Billy better get used to it. Change is unavoidable.

Change is a constant, and it is entirely unavoidable. See it, and accept it. This will save you a lot of stress if you listen.

Let not your mind run on what you lack as much as on what you have already.

Appreciation is key.

You can make yourself absolutely miserable if you focus on what other people have that you do not have.

This is where so many people in capitalist societies focus on which draws them into socialist worldviews. They claim to want to help the poor, but if you listen closely you will see clearly that they don't give a damn about the poor, they just hate the rich.

Thinking only of what you do not have is a terrible way to go through life. It is far better to appreciate what you have and to find ways to use what you have to make those you care about happy and safe.

If it is not right do not do it; if it is not true do not say it.

Everyone does things that they know they should not do. It is a man's task to limit this behavior.

Maybe you eat too much, or swear too much, or are dishonest in your business dealings, or are unfaithful to your Wife. Correct this <u>now</u>.

Stop doing the things that you know are wrong, and you will be amazed at the improvement in your life.

And stop telling untruths. This is difficult because it is human nature to try to always present ourselves in the best possible light, but this is a habit that must be overcome.

Start right now, in this moment.

I have often wondered how it is that every man loves himself more than all the rest of men, but yet sets less value on his own opinions of himself than on the opinions of others.

You will never be valued in the eyes of others in the way that you want to be valued. Period.

Human nature being what it is, you will find that other people always secretly care less for you than you would wish.

Instead of placing such value on their opinions, make yourself into the person that you most want to be, others will like you or they won't, but you will respect yourself, and this is a key essential in bringing out the best of yourself.

Set your sights on being a good man. The definition of what is a good man will vary person to person, but you will still understand. Be the best man that you can be and everything else will fall into place.

Consider that before long you will be nobody and

nowhere, nor will any of the things exist that you now see, nor any of those who are now living. For all things are formed by nature to change and be turned and to perish in order that other things in continuous succession may exist.

It is easy to trick yourself into thinking that you will live forever and that age, sickness, and death will not come to you. But eventually we all are divested of this false notion.

Rather than a notion of "all is lost", see this as a stress on the importance of making what good you can of the time you have. Be the best person you can be, and have a meaningful impact on the lives of those around you.

Be a blessing to them, and see that they are to you as well.

Look for the best, and be prepared for the opposite.

If you always expect the worst from people, you are going to leave them with no reason to be good to you.

However, even though you do not want to be caught off guard, so it is necessary to look for the best, hope for it and seek it out. But it is equally necessary to be prepared to deal with the worst should it happen.

There is no harm is looking for the best in people and situations. This is simply a matter of being good and looking for good.

It is true that, with most people, they will strive to be better when they know that someone is thinking highly of them and expecting the best. There are some who are slackers in this regard, but they are in the minority. Most people try harder for people who believe in them.

At the same time, you have to be prepared and have a plan of action for when people fail you. And make no mistake, some people will fail you.

Try not to be judgmental in these instances. Many people have simply had the line dropped on them so many times that they gave up on themselves, and no amount of faith placed in them will bring them to a point where they believe in themselves again.

Do the best that you can. It is a true balancing act.

Be content to seem what you really are.

In our time, the number of people who have an alternate, cyber-self that is little more than a caricature of a character is staggering.

People seem to get an idea of what they think they are supposed to be, based on what they are told to be by whatever media source they trust, and then they try to give this *self* a form of cyber-reality.

This is insanity.

Who you really are matters more than your political ideology, preferred musical genre, skin color, or any of the other seemingly infinite ways in which people want to divide themselves into little in-groups and out-groups.

Grow up and be yourself.

You have power over your mind – not outside events. Realize this, and you will find strength.

Again, we see a return to the thought that we have limited control of much of life. This one contains a reminder that we do have control over our mind. Exercise that control.

The mind works strangely. We can see a social media post and, with no evidence whatsoever, decide that the person was posting about us.

This is, unfortunately, normal in our time. But does it make any sense at all?

When your mind is painting false realities and giving them life, remind yourself that things are not always about you, and that sometimes we can read too much into anything.

The best revenge is not to be like your enemy.

How many times have you seen it happen in politics, where one party will attack the excesses of the other, and eventually convince a majority of the people into putting them in power, only to end up becoming just as corrupt as the people they replaced? Rather than seeking the mere defeat of your foes, regardless of cost, focus on what makes your point of view the right one.

This comes down to the idea of placing values ahead of issues.

It is sad to say, but in the modern times, the media cannot be trusted, regardless of your trusted media source.

News media is a business, and they rely on advertisement revenue. As such, they must bend to the will and ideals of their advertisers. You are no longer being informed by news media, you are being influenced.

Live by your code, and do not allow outside influences to shape you or your opinions. Make up your own mind. Do not be like those you claim to oppose.

Confine yourself to the present.

Much like the Zen maxim of *be here now*, this is

about shutting down the constant distractions that you mind can come up with for entertainment.

Here is a simple task, try to hear tomorrow, anything tomorrow.

Can you do it?

No you cannot.

What about yesterday, can you hear it with your ears?

No, again, you cannot. It is simply not there through the sense of your hearing.

Can you see tomorrow?

Same thing, you cannot.

Can you see yesterday with your eyes?

You cannot.

The past and the future are simply not there according to your basic senses. The past exists in memory alone. The future exists only in anticipation and imagination. Be here, where you are, right now.

This now is all that there is to the plain experience of your senses. In this, you will feel a lot of worry fall away.

When you arise in the morning, think of what a precious privilege it is to be alive – to breathe, to think, to enjoy, to love.

For anyone who has lost friends and family, or even come close to losing their own life, life itself has a sweetness to it that cannot be duplicated or explained to those who have not shared such experiences. But even more, there is a deep appreciation for life itself that is gained through these terrible experiences.

It is a truly great thing to know when you are happy, and it is better still to be able to find great joy in simple things.

Waste no more time arguing about what a good man should be. Be one.

We can argue and debate what qualities do or do not make a man good. And this is not really a bad thing, but it is better still to actually *be* a good man.

In the end, that is what matters. If men as a whole would simply be a good man, and ignore the nonsense about toxic this and misogynist that, follow the traditions that have been handed down to us as a birthright, we can turn things around in short order.

Notes: Marcus Aurelius was a unique person. He

was a master of many facets of thinking, philosophy, leadership, and so much more.

Marcus saw no limits on what he was to be, he simply did what men do when they see things clearly.

We can do this too in our time, if we are but willing to do so. We can meet our obligations head on, face our challenges and overcome them, fight the good fight.

In life we win some and lose some.

From victory we learn to be humble, and from loss we learn to survive being bested.

Nothing that happens to us in this life *has* to make us into a bad person. Regardless of outside circumstances, we all have the option to do what is right.

To be a man in the fullest sense, we need to understand that there are things that we will go through that damage us, and we must press forward.

Our personal hurts do not relieve us of our responsibilities. There are things that must be done, and sometimes our feelings do not count.

In truth, *most* of the time our feelings and our pain

are completely irrelevant.

One of the biggest issues that young people in our time face is the stark contrast between the way children are currently raised, where they are the absolute center of the universe and they are (told they are) perfect in every way, yet when they become adults they are forced to deal with the fact that the rest of the world couldn't care any less about them.

This is bound to cause anyone some difficulties.

As men, we must help those who were raised this way to see things correctly. We can help the younger generation to learn how to cope.

In doing so, we can help to ensure that the blood of our Fathers was not shed in vain.

THE BLOOD OF OUR FATHERS

14 Conclusion

Throughout this book we have seen a variety of thought regarding the different codes of ethics a man might apply to his approach to life.

We have looked into the wisdom of several warrior cultures and tried to see what knowledge the modern man might take from the cultures of heroes.

We have also looked into the writings of a few badass men in the hope of finding a clue as to how they discovered the path that made them who they were.

In the end, as in the beginning, we are on our own.

Men have to be okay with that in our time.

We no longer have a culture that fosters the best in us that men can be, instead we have a culture that beats us down, hoping to beat us into submission. We are supposed to say that the world is bad because men were in charge of so much for so long, and that the world and humanity would be better off if not for the existence of men.

Of course, this is complete nonsense.

The inconvenient fact is that many societies throughout history were led by men because *it worked.*

This in no way insinuates that women were incapable of leadership, even though the words will be taken to mean that by people who have nothing better to do than find fault with anything and everything that goes against the anti-male agenda of the modern feminist movement.

It is, rather, to say that throughout human history, people have done the best that they could do. There never was an intent to suppress women, only an intent to protect the tribe, clan, family, or nation. An intent to *survive.*

So, if we are clear about our intentions here, what sort of takeaway do we have from this book?

Even with a passing glance, it is easy to see that many of the virtues held in reverence by warriors and warrior cultures overlap one another. There is a lot of repetition chapter to chapter.

This tells us that certain values were nearly universally important.

If we are to take the book as a whole, we can see that this is a great point of departure for anyone looking to find the best code of ethics for their own use.

We can, and we possibly *must* develop a certain set of guidelines that we, as men, can follow and teach to the younger generations.

Many boys today have no Father at home to guide them in how to be a good man. Someone must fill in that gap, or the boys will find someone to fill the role for them.

What would we list as indispensable qualities of manhood?

We can start with the obvious, *responsibility*.

A child, when caught doing something that they know they are not supposed to do, will first lie. This is an attempt at avoiding responsibility for their actions, and this is a habit that is supposed to be outgrown.

Men should be responsible for their words and their actions. If you make a mistake, own it! Do what needs to be done to remedy or correct the situation as best you can, but never deny your part of what occurred.

It is easy to accept the praise for what you do right, but those things you do that are wrong, sometimes it is difficult to let it be known. And some mistakes can carry consequences that will last for years.

Other times, we might not necessarily make a

mistake, but we make choices that affect the lives of other people, such as helping to create a child. There is a responsibility in Fatherhood that is frightening to many men, but we must take that responsibility and bear it. When we are talking about something that impacts the lives of others, we really need to be a man about it and be responsible.

There is a sense of shame that we all have. But this sense of shame is supposed to be a guide to doing what is right, and we only know this if we have ever been taught this.

If you are afraid of being responsible then you are a child and not a man.

If you know better, then do better.

It sounds so easy that it is almost stupid to include it here. But it is included here *because* so many men do not see this as an issue.

Back in the early 2000s, I lost control of my eating habits. Or maybe I didn't care what happened to me at the time, or I didn't care if I died, I am not really sure.

But the point is that I ate a *lot* of fast food, and my weight ballooned. My weight peaked at 320 lbs. My blood pressure was out of control, my health was failing, and I could not climb the stairs to bed without using my arms to help pull up my ample frame.

I was eating a near fatal dose of sodium every single day at lunch.

Eventually, other health problems caused me to be unable to eat the way I was eating, and the weight began to drop. When the weight went down, exercising became easier. The weight dropped faster.

While I am not now, and never will be the picture of great health, I did manage to drop 70 lbs.

I dropped the weight when I stopped doing the things that I knew I shouldn't be doing. You can improve your life the same way.

And it doesn't have to be anything earth shattering. Small changes are easiest to make, and often they are the gateway to greater changes.

If you have a bad habit, and you know you do, break it.

You are a man, for God's sake, do what needs to be done.

Be a provider.

Notice I did not say that you need to be *the* provider.

Do the work. Be industrious. Get out and bring home some bacon. I don't know any man today who has a problem with his Wife earning more money than he does, but every man I know who does not work and is supported by someone else, whether it be his Wife or the government, is totally miserable and hates himself.

Do *something*.

There are a lot of people who will tell you that *if you love your job, you never work a day in your life.* Well, that is pure unadulterated, Grade A, free-range, grass fed, organic, boneless BS.

I love my job more than anyone that you will ever know loves their job, and the fact is that there are times when my job wears me down to the point of mental and physical exhaustion. Just like nearly every person you will ever meet.

Work isn't supposed to be your point of joy; that is why we call it work! Work is how you do your part to provide for your family.

If you approach it with the attitude of taking care of those you love, the work itself will become more bearable, even if it is not your favorite of all possible jobs. And in the best cases, you work will even become enjoyable, it all depends on where you choose to place your focus.

For years, I worked as a stone mason. The work was very physically demanding. I never liked being a mason, but it paid better than anything else I could find to do, so it was a mason's life for me!

I hated the work, but I liked the money, so I did it. After I was married and became a Father, the outlook with which I approached work changed.

When I was responsible only to myself, I left employers anytime I wanted a break. I was good enough at what I did that I knew that they would hire me back anytime, and I never had trouble finding a new employer when I had had enough time off.

Once I had real responsibilities to my Wife and Children, this changed. I stopped leaving employers at will, and was there every day that they wanted me to be there. Things really got better when I had a chance to move to the Dallas area and work for Chuck Norris' *Kickstart Kids*. But the real point of departure for the change was my attitude toward my work.

Be a real Dad to your kids.

If you willingly helped to create the child, and I am *sure* you were not forced, then you need to own up to the responsibilities that go along with that.

One of the biggest facts thrown in the face of men by women who hate men is the staggering number of deadbeat dads. Those idiotic men who help make a baby, and then try to leave the women to do all of the baby raising on her own. This kind of pathetic behavior needs to stop. And if it does stop, then one of the strongest points of contention against men will go away.

One of the easiest ways to figure out your role as a Dad is to make the child the center of your life. Even if things didn't work out with the Mother, this is not the fault of the child, and this in no way relieves you of your responsibilities to the child.

All children *need* a positive male role model in their life. This is as true today as it has been in traditional societies throughout history.

The boys need to see how a real man is supposed to act, react, and navigate life.

The girls need to see how a real man is supposed to treat them.

You cannot do this if you walk out of their life. And even this speaks nothing to the impact the child will have on those in their life.

Without that positive role model, they will go through life and spread their negative worldview.

With the positive role model, they can make their

own positive impacts on the lives of others.

It isn't only about you. Do not allow yourself to begin to think that it is.

While I am on the subject...

Tend to others.

A man has to be able to think of others and what they need. This is the driving force behind all of the talk in the chapters that included brotherhood as a value to ponder.

You will find out at some point in your life that you have relatives, those whose lives you were born into. You had no choice in the matter, and only your parents played any role at all in your coming into being.

But as you grow older, you will have those in your life that you chose to keep. These people are family, and they matter a lot.

In everyone's life, there is triumph and trial. We all go through ups and downs. But unless you are new to this world, you will have already discovered that having a person there who cares enough to ask you if you are okay can make all of the difference in the world.

You are not the center of the universe. Look out for your family. Take care of them when they need it. Check on them. There is no loss of manhood in asking a friend if they are okay. And it can make a tremendous difference for them.

All men have a chance to be the person that they needed to have when they hit their low point. Help when you can.

Develop the ability to protect those you love.

Not every man is going to be a great warrior, but we are all equipped to be warriors, great or otherwise depends upon training and playing to our own strengths.

If you are physically gifted, or not so much, *play to your strengths*. If you are able to fight physically, train and learn all you can on that front.

If you are less naturally gifted, then you might need to seek an alternative. If they are legal where you live, firearms are a great equalizer. You do not have to be physically imposing, and the training to become proficient is much less rigorous than training in the martial arts.

If you are minded for it, training in bladed weapon arts is deadly when taught and trained properly. If you ever have to use it, things will be a bloody mess, but the effectiveness of a blade against bare hands is undeniable.

We, as men, have an obligation as well as an

instinct to protect those whom we love. We need to accept this obligation, embrace it, and become capable of fulfilling it to the best of our ability.

My best recommendation on this front, find a martial art that suits your physicality, train in that thoroughly, and learn to fight in the ranges not covered by that art. Then, train in blade and gun.

We do not need to be violent men, but we do need to be good men who are capable of great violence. In this way we can protect those who are counting on us, should the need ever arrive.

Don't whine.

When I was a teen, there was a song that became popular titled *We've got a five dollar fine for whining.* My Father liked it so much he would admonish us and tell us to pay five dollars if he thought we were whining about anything.

Complaints are really just a lot of whining. When a woman whines, she is playing a role that activates our protection response. When a man whines…

As a man, there will be a growing list of aches and pains, and we will never feel that we are treated with the proper respect at home or at work.

Learn to deal with this in silence.

And if you need some perspective on this, think of someone you know who is a whiner. They are pretty annoying people and you probably don't enjoy being around them, right?

Well, that is precisely what other people are thinking about you when you start to whine.

What matters most is doing what is right. Not the accolades, not what the people in charge notice, not even being noticed at all. The *action* is what matters and it is all that we can give the world.

Participate in competitive sports.

Men *need* competition. It is in our DNA.

A lot of what is happening to the young men in our world today has a lot to do with the removal of competition from the lives of our children.

The motive for this removal sounded so good-hearted and so pure that only a crass, boorish chowderhead would ever speak out against it; "losing hurts a child's feelings".

We do not want children to suffer the pain of losing in a sporting event, or facing up to the fact that they are not as athletically talented (or is it hard-working) as the next kid. We don't want it, but losing is an immeasurably important lesson in life. It hurts, but it can motivate, when properly framed. It can bring us to put forth greater effort the next time.

Not all negative experiences are damaging, and losing in a sporting event is certainly not as traumatic as people tell themselves that it is. And it is certainly not traumatic to boys. The male is hardwired for competition.

If you think that competitive drive is not hardwired into the male brain, I suggest you ride with a 19-year old driver. You will lose this delusion very quickly.

Sports offer several benefits to the young male. There is, obviously, competition. There is a chance to release competitive aggression, young men *need* that. There is also the camaraderie, the brotherhood. Young men need that too. And they need time to be spent under the eye of an older male. Kids who do not experience good coaching, which will *necessarily* involve being told when they are flat out doing terrible and that they need to work harder, will do poorly as an adult.

For those men reading this who are already grown, I recommend finding a sport to participate in. Anything from martial arts to golf, auto racing to tennis. Even older men need a chance to be competitively aggressive. We tend to only do this at work, but we need other outlets as well. Sports can give us this outlet.

Which leads me to the next point.

Get in shape.

Our day and age has luxuries which our forebears could never have even imagined. We have the ability to find out any trivial fact or important information in an instant. We can make friends across the globe and never have an actual face-to-face conversation with them. We can start our vehicles by remote and have the heater or A/C adjust the temperature just where we want it before we get to our car.

This has led to many less than optimal lifestyle options. We can go to work, never break a sweat and never get up off of our asses until it is time to go eat. And then we will go eat a lunch containing more calories that we burn in a week, which we will follow up by returning to our desk where we sit and do nothing.

It is difficult for some people to sacrifice screen time in order to put in some exercise, but this *must* be done. We think it is impossible for a person to die of heart failure when they are still in their 20s, but I can sadly assure you that it happens.

In more traditional societies, men were moving so much and doing so many strenuous activities during a normal day that this was not an issue.

But times have changed.

The sedentary lifestyle is terrible for our health, and when the stress we endure is taken into account, we see a recipe for disaster.

Eating right is necessary, but exercise is paramount.

Physiologically speaking, men *need* to get up and move around. Our chemistry demands it even when our minds want to stare at a screen.

Start an exercise program, *any* exercise program. You will notice a difference in how good you feel within the first few days, if not sooner.

This, coupled with the training in being a protector will make you physically capable of protecting your home and family. You need to be fighting fit.

There are a lot of people in the martial arts community who tout the fact that real fights do not tend to last very long, and I will not argue with them on this point, they are right. But the factor that is ignored in the assertion is that real fights, although not lasting very long, are incredibly intense.

Being fighting fit is absolutely mandatory if we are to be the protector that we were born to be.

You really do have to take care of yourself before you can take care of others. The airlines all remind us of this when they tell us on every flight that if the oxygen masks drop down, our first action is to put our own mask on, and then help those around us if they need help. Getting in shape is a huge chunk of taking care of yourself, and you do not need to make excuses, just get out there and get it done.

Be better than they think.

In the modern wave of the feminist movement, there is almost no talk of raising the status of women, only of the evils of men.

They will say in all seriousness that every man is a potential rapist. They will say that men tried, throughout history, to keep women down. They will say that men want to make babies but not raise them.

Prove them wrong.

Regardless of the volumes that could be filled with the lies told about men, most men would never harm a woman. Most men want to be a part of the life of their child, and most men support the equal opportunity for women at all levels. It seems suspicious to me that with so many men supporting the feminist agenda at one point, that the agenda suddenly changed into something that no sane man could support.

To be sure, you can find male liberal arts

professors who will say that men are evil, just as you can find white male liberal arts professors who offer the idea that white genocide would be a good thing, there is always going to be someone who follow what they see as the "in crowd". But by and large, men cannot get behind the philosophy that we are evil.

But we need not take on the hideous attitudes of those who want to tear us down. We can prove them wrong by being better than they say we are.

Fulfill your role, be the protector of home and family, give them food and shelter, and just be a man.

You are not going to make those who hate us for being born male ever decide that they like you, so just be the best that you can be, and leave the rest alone.

This does not mean that you will suddenly become perfect. But if you are true to your code, you can be a genuinely good person, and they will have a very hard time ripping you apart.

Be willing to fight.

We have all heard the old and tired line about how "violence is never the answer". What we do not always notice is the addendum typically placed after the statement, "Violence is never the answer, unless someone is hurting my child".

That added section of the statement renders the first part void. If violence is never the answer, unless blah blah blah, then violence sometimes *actually is* the answer.

The modern man has his more violent impulses shamed out of him, for the most part. Many of us simply do not talk about these impulses, but we know they exist. We know that if needed, men who are willing to fight will suddenly become acceptable.

We need to be that man. The blood of our Fathers was not shed so that we could become a bunch of frightened children, cowering in terror over mean words.

Our predecessors fought and died that others might live. They died so that their sons might take up arms in their stead, and that their daughters would be protected.

We men are, first and foremost, the protectors. As stated before, we need to get the training to fulfill this role, and we need to get fighting fit for the same reason.

But we also need to have the ability to flip that switch that we have inside of our minds that allows us to give ourselves permission to be violent.

And it is this switch that makes us different from what the naysayers claim about men.

A savage is a person who has no control over their violent impulses.

A terrorist is someone who has control over these impulses, but chooses to use them to kill and scare people.

A man is someone who has the ability and the willingness to commit violence, but chooses the when and where of this action based on circumstances and his code of conduct.

Being willing to use violence to stop the bad guy in no way makes us bad men. Quite the opposite! It makes us very good men.

In the end, after all of the pontificating about how men should be nice in order to not scare the sheep, when the predator comes to the door, only someone who is willing and able to out-violence the bad guy will be able to stop the bad guy.

People can debate the details all that they want, but generations of good men were able to be violent when necessary, and peaceful at all other times, and they didn't succeed by sitting around brooding on the right and wrong of violence itself.

Violence is not always the only option, but there is no debating the point that there are times when it is the best option.

Being willing to be the man to step up and risk his very life to save the lives of those he loves is a statement on the price you are willing to pay to fulfill your role, and it speaks volumes on the depth of love.

Forget entitlement.

No one owes you anything. If you want something, set your mind to working and earning it.

As a teen I wanted a vehicle more than I could ever hope to describe here. But, being born into a poor family, I did not have the funds to buy anything. So I did what people in my generation did, I worked and I saved.

My first vehicle was a 1967 Chevy truck. I had four on the floor with a low granny, and it came with a built in transmission problem. It had terrible flaking paint, and it was a visual nightmare, but it was mine all mine.

I had a pride in owning this rattling old truck because of how hard I had to work to get it. The same goes for everything that I ever got in life that I had to work for.

Earning a Black Belt is in the same category. I am not athletically gifted. I have always been injury-prone. I never had a lot of money. I have a love for food that exceeds reason. Becoming a black belt is not something that should have been possible for me, and yet I have managed to gain instructor rank in several systems.

No one did it for me, and I didn't reach rank simply by showing up. It was work, a lot of work and sweat and sometimes blood. And because of all of this, it means a lot to me.

Working and earning what you want will also give you an unexpected benefit; gratefulness.

Being grateful is the real key to happiness. From the poorest to the richest, you will find that those who are happiest are those who are grateful for what they have. You can be happy too by learning to appreciate what you have and not waiting for someone to just give you a handout.

Live as an example.

So many young men in our time do not have any positive example to follow. They have celebrities who exploit their positions of influence in order to make money, at the expense of those who are following their example. They have whiny, spoiled brat athletes who set a very poor standard of conduct.

Break this cycle by being someone that the young men can aspire to be like. Do the right thing, even when it isn't the easy thing.

You never know who is watching you; how you act, how you react, what you choose to do with spare time, how you treat other men, how you treat women, if your word means anything, what your work ethic is, what loyalty means to you, what family means to you, who you show respect to, and who you do not, and on and on.

There is a high likelihood that a young man watching, and your actions probably influence his behavior and choices a lot more than you know. Make sure that your influence is a positive one.

***

We men are not as bad as what our modern society is claiming, but we are also not living up to our full potential.

We have the power to change this.

In all traditional societies men had a code of ethics to live by. These codes were handed down one generation to the next. And that was a system that worked fine for a very long time.

Fast-forward to our time and it is obvious what happens to a society that does not follow this practice.

Set this aside. It doesn't do any good to pout

about what our culture no longer practices.

Instead of brooding, look to what can be done. Be a problem solver. Waste no energy on lamenting the lack of a good code of conduct in our day and age to teach young men to be the best that they can be.

Instead, *BE* that good man.

And maybe then, just maybe, we will be allowed to return to that neighborhood park. Maybe the boy playing as Batman will be allowed to pretend he is a hero. Maybe the boys playing at war might learn to protect. And maybe the boys playing basketball will be allowed to just play and compete with each other.

And maybe we can just let them play.

ABOUT THE AUTHOR

Wallace Smedley has trained in martial arts since 1983 and is currently a 6th degree Black Belt. He has extensive experience in both western and eastern martial arts ranging from western boxing and wrestling to Chinese and Korean martial arts.

Wallace has worked for Chuck Norris' Kickstart Kids Foundation since 2002. As a part of this work he teaches karate as an alternate P.E. credit elective class. During his time with Kickstart Kids he has had the opportunity to work with more than 1,000 students and that number continues to grow. Kickstart Kids is a character education program that uses karate as a tool to recruit and retain students. Working inside of the public school system, and side-by-side with other education professionals he had the opportunity to learn how to teach like a teacher while instilling the character strengths that will allow these students to become contributors to society.

Beginning in 2012 he took on the additional responsibilities by accepting a position as an Area Leader for Kickstart Kids, which allowed him to also help other Kickstart Kids Instructors better implement the teaching methods in the classroom. He also served on a committee that was charged with creating and developing the Character Education Values Curriculum for the Foundation.

He has written hundreds of articles and published several books on the traditional martial arts, practical application of martial arts, as well as the subject of personal safety. His books *Slapping Dragons, Ignorance, Myth and the Martial Arts,* and *Texas Hold'em Self-Defense* were all well received and in 2019 he will be releasing *Texas Rattlesnake Kung Fu.*

He lives in the Dallas/Fort Worth area of north Texas. Hunting and fishing are a big part of his life. He takes online MOOC courses as a part of his philosophy that learning never stops, and enjoys any and every free moment with his Wife, Daisy, and their children, Gillian, and Ysabella. He offers this book in the memory of his Son, CJ, who passed away on October 19, 2017.

He can always be reached at smedleymartialarts@gmail.com, or through his blog at wallacesmedley.com and he welcomes feedback from his readers.

Also by Wallace Smedley:

Slapping Dragons:

All too often, martial artists surrender their intellectual freedom and opt instead to accept without thinking the strange and unbelievable claims made by so-called masters and experts in the martial arts. Wallace Smedley takes a close look at the claims and asks important questions about the basis for such acceptance. Some of the claims are harmless, but some can get you killed if you follow them, and so questions need to be asked. Often, asking questions on the subjects can be compared to slapping a dragon, but Smedley claims that there are times when Slapping Dragons is exactly what we need to do. This book contains expanded articles comprised from the best of wallacesmedley.com as well as new material.

This one was my first non "how to" book. It was well received and I am quite proud of the success and well as the lessons learned.

Ignorance, Myth, and the Martial Arts:

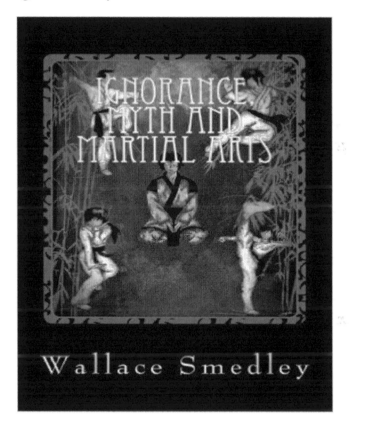

Within the martial arts a person will find outrageous claims, and subtle lies. There are tales of ancient masters who had powers usually reserved for Superman or Santa Clause, but there are also instructors who use misleading marketing tactics to entice students to pay to be safe. Few instructors actually tell students that the best way to be safe is to be nice to people and not act like a raving ding-dong anytime someone rubs you the wrong way. One will also find absurd practices and a near brainwashing process where you surrender your critical thinking in favor of herd mentality. It is easy to not question the instructor, or the procedures and policies of the class and organization. There is a much more difficult road in questioning, but questions must be asked.

Texas Hold'em Self Defense:

Every single day across this country people are taught ways to save their life from the bad guy, only to end up in jail for assault if their training works as advertised. They are taught to gamble their life and freedom on what they are told is fact.

Self-defense is not like high stakes gambling, it is the highest stakes gambling.

If you are going to gamble - do it right. To do it right you need to know how the game is played, what the rules are, and you really need to understand the odds.

That is where this book comes in. Texas Hold'em Self-Defense will teach you how to play the game, how much it costs, and how to turn the odds in your favor.

References:

Beck, Paul N. (2013). Columns of Vengeance: Soldiers, Sioux, and the Punitive Expeditions, 1863-1864. Norman, OK: University of Oklahoma Press.

Christafferson, Dennis M. (2001). "Sioux, 1930–2000". In R. J. DeMallie (Ed.), Handbook of North American Indians: Plains (Vol. 13, Part 2, pp. 821–839). W. C. Sturtevant Washington, D.C.: Smithsonian Institution. ISBN 0-16-050400-7.

DeMallie, Raymond J. (2001a). "Sioux until 1850". In R. J. DeMallie (Ed.), Handbook of North American Indians: Plains (Vol. 13, Part 2, pp. 718–760). W. C. Sturtevant Washington, D.C.: Smithsonian Institution. ISBN 0-16-050400-7.

DeMallie, Raymond J. (2001b). "Teton". In R. J. DeMallie (Ed.), Handbook of North American Indians: Plains (Vol. 13, Part 2, pp. 794–820). W. C. Sturtevant Smithsonian Institution. ISBN 0-16-050400-7.

Matson, William and Frethem, Mark (2006). Producers. "The Authorized Biography of Crazy Horse and His Family Part One: Creation, Spirituality, and the Family Tree". The Crazy Horse family tells their oral history and with explanations of Lakota spirituality and culture on DVD. (Publisher is Reelcontact.com)

Parks, Douglas R.; & Rankin, Robert L. (2001). "The Siouan Languages". In R. J. DeMallie (Ed.), Handbook of North American Indians: Plains (Vol. 13, Part 1, pp. 94–114). W. C. Sturtevant (Gen. Ed.). Washington,

D.C.: Smithsonian Institution. ISBN 978-0-16-050400-6.
Pritzker, Barry M. A Native American Encyclopedia:
History, Culture, and Peoples. Oxford: Oxford
University Press, 2000. ISBN 978-0-19-513877-1.
Ullrich, Jan. (2011) New Lakota Dictionary. Lakota
Language Consortium. ISBN 0-9761082-9-1. Henning,
Stanley (1994), "Ignorance, Legend and Taijiquan"
(PDF), Journal of the Chenstyle Taijiquan Research
Association of Hawaii, 2 (3): 1–7

Henning, Stan; Green, Tom (2001), Folklore in the
Martial Arts. In: Green, Thomas A., "Martial Arts of
the World: An Encyclopedia", Santa Barbara, Calif:
ABC-CLIO

Lin, Boyuan (1996), Zhōngguó wǔshù shǐ 中國武術史,
Taipei 臺北: Wǔzhōu chūbǎnshè 五洲出版社

Ryuchi, Matsuda 松田隆智 (1986), Zhōngguó wǔshù
shǐlüè 中國武術史略 (in Chinese), Taipei 臺北: Danqing
tushu

Shahar, Meir (2008), The Shaolin Monastery: history,
religion, and the Chinese martial arts, University of
Hawaii Press, ISBN 978-0-8248-3110-3. Davies,
Norman (1997) [1996]. Europe: a History. Random
House. ISBN 0712666338.

Adcock, F.E. (1957), The Greek and Macedonian Art of
War, Berkeley: University of California Press, ISBN 0-
520-00005-6

Autenrieth, Georg (1891). A Homeric Dictionary for

Schools and Colleges. New York: Harper and Brothers.

Bradford, Ernle (2004), Thermopylae: The Battle for the West, New York: Da Capo Press, ISBN 0-306-81360-2

Buxton, Richard (1999), From Myth to Reason?: Studies in the Development of Greek Thought, Oxford: Clarendon Press, ISBN 0-7534-5110-7

Cartledge, Paul (2002), Sparta and Lakonia: A Regional History 1300 to 362 BC (2 ed.), Oxford: Routledge, ISBN 0-415-26276-3

Cartledge, Paul (2001), Spartan Reflections, London: Duckworth, ISBN 0-7156-2966-2

Cartledge, Paul. "What have the Spartans Done for us?: Sparta's Contribution to Western Civilization", Greece & Rome, Vol. 51, Issue 2 (2004), pp. 164–179.

Cartledge, Paul; Spawforth, Antony (2001), Hellenistic and Roman Sparta (2 ed.), Oxford: Routledge, ISBN 0-415-26277-1

Ehrenberg, Victor (1973), From Solon to Socrates: Greek History and Civilisation between the 6th and 5th centuries BC (2 ed.), London: Routledge, ISBN 0-415-04024-8

Forrest, W.G. (1968), A History of Sparta, 950–192 B.C., New York: W. W. Norton & Co.

Green, Peter (1998), The Greco-Persian Wars (2 ed.), Berkeley: University of California Press, ISBN 0-520-20313-5

Liddell, Henry George; Scott, Robert (1940). Jones, Henry Stuart, ed. A Greek-English Lexicon. Oxford: Clarendon Press

Morris, Ian (1992), Death-Ritual and Social Structure in Classical Antiquity, Cambridge: Cambridge University Press, ISBN 0-521-37611-4

Pomeroy, Sarah B. (2002), Spartan Women, Oxford: Oxford University Press, ISBN 978-0-19-513067-6

Powell, Anton (2001), Athens and Sparta: Constructing Greek Political and Social History from 478 BC (2 ed.), London: Routledge, ISBN 0-415-26280-1

Pausanias (1918). Description of Greece. with an English Translation by W.H.S. Jones, Litt.D., and H.A. Ormerod, M.A., in 4 Volumes. Cambridge, MA; London.

Plutarch (1874), Plutarch's Morals, Plutarch, William W. Goodwin, PH. D., Boston, Cambridge

Plutarch (1891), Bernardakis, Gregorius N., ed., Moralia, Plutarch (in Greek), Leipzig: Teubner

Plutarch (2005), Richard J.A. Talbert, ed., On Sparta (2 ed.), London: Penguin Books, ISBN 0-14-044943-4

Plutarch (2004), Frank Cole Babbitt, ed., Moralia Vol. III, Loeb Classical Library, Cambridge: Harvard University Press, ISBN 0-674-99270-9

Thompson, F. Hugh (2002), The Archaeology of Greek and Roman Slavery, London: Duckworth, ISBN 0-7156-3195-0

Thucydides (1974), M.I. Finley, Rex Warner, ed., History of the Peloponnesian War, London: Penguin Books, ISBN 0-14-044039-9

West, M.L. (1999), Greek Lyric Poetry, Oxford: Oxford University Press, ISBN 978-0-19-954039-6 Toyota

Masataka. "Niten Ki (A Chronicle of Two Heavens)", in Gorin no Sho, ed. Kamiko Tadashi (Tokyo: Tokuma-shoten, 1963), 239.

Miyamoto Musashi. "Go Rin No Sho", in Gorin no Sho, ed. Kamiko Tadashi (Tokyo: Tokuma-shoten, 1963),

Kenji Tokitsu (2004). Miyamoto Musashi: His Life and Writings. Shambhala.

Brant, Miyamoto Musashi; translated by Ashikaga Yoshiharu; edited by Rosemary (2006). The Book of Five Rings: the classic text of Samurai sword strategy New York: Barnes & Noble. ISBN 978-0-7607-8457-0.

Harris, Victor, p. 10, Miyamoto p. 16.

William Scott Wilson. (2004). The Lone Samurai. Kodansha International. ISBN 978-4-7700-2942-3.

Toyota, p. 250

Almo, Leif (founder). "Musashi Miyamoto - the Legend". Kendo.com. Scandnet AB.

http://www.hyoho.com Hayakutake-Watkin

"What Is a Gunslinger?". Wisegeek. September 22, 2014

Chuck Parsons, Clay Allison: Portrait of a Shootist (Seagraves, Texas: Pioneer, 1983)

Bishop, William Henry (1888). Old Mexico and her Lost Provinces: a Journey in Mexico, Southern California.

Tim Dirks. "Western Films Part 1". Filmsite.org.

H. Lo. "What Are the Characteristics of the Western Genre?"

Miss Cellania. "The Truth About Gunfights in the Old

West". Neutorama. June 7, 2012

"Old West Legends". Legends of America.

Adams, Cecil. "Did Western gunfighters really face off one-on-one?". Straight Dope.

"MythBusters: Hollywood Gunslingers". Discovery Channel.

Ed McGivern's Book of Fast and Fancy Revolver Shooting. Skyhorse Publishing Inc. ISBN 978-1-60239-086-7.(2007) pp. 101–103

"Old West Myths ... And Things Little Known". Shotdoc.com.

McLachlan, Sean (2013). Tombstone – Wyatt Earp, the O.K. Corral, and the Vendetta Ride 1881–82. Osprey Publishing. p. 50. ISBN 978-1-78096-194-1. Retrieved 2 August 2013.

Ayoob, Massad (September–October 2006). "Frontier Style Handguns For The Modern Backwoods Home". Backwoods Home Magazine.

Fournier, Richard. "Mexican War Vet Wages Deadliest Gunfight in American History", VFW Magazine (January 2012), p. 30.

"An Outlaw's Arsenal". American Experience.

"Wild bill vs Tutt duel". Spartacus Educational.

"The Indian Wars". Boundless.

Cellania, Miss. "The Meanest Towns in the West". Neotorama.

"The Law in Tombstone".

Petzal, David. "Five Greatest Gunfights of the Old West". Field and Stream.

Tombstone Nugget; October 27, 1881 article

El Paso Times article documenting the event

Raynor, Jessica. "Billy Dixon". Amarillo.com. Retrieved April 19, 2014.

Clayburn, Glenn (September 12, 2013). "6 Real-Life Gunslingers Who Put Billy the Kid to Shame". Cracked. "Wild Bill Hickok fights first western showdown". History.com.

"Politics And Pistols: Dueling In America". History Detectives. PBS.

Wyatt-Brown, Bertram. 1982. Southern Honor: Ethics and Behavior in the Old South. New York: Oxford University Press. Pages 167 and 350-351. ISBN 0195325176

Bell, Bob Boze. "Wyatt Goes Rogue". True West Magazine. Archived from the original on December 22, 2014.

Isenberg, Andrew C. (2013). Wyatt Earp: A Vigilante Life. Hill and Wang; First Edition. p. Chapter 4: Jerk Your. ISBN 978-0809095001. Retrieved 18 October 2014.

"This Day in History: Doc Holliday". History.com.

"Gunfighters Part 4". Legends of America.

"Gunfights: Long Branch Saloon Shootout". Legends of America. Archived from the original on 2008-03-21.

"Jim Levy - The Jewish Gunfighter". Legends of America.

Shoot-out (1877) Old West Gunfights - Page 2 Archived 2012-07-19 at the Wayback Machine.

Legends of America

Grady, David P. (July–August 1996). "American Cowboy". American Cowboy: 64. Retrieved 28 June 2012.

Desert Evening News November 20, 1903

McGrath, Roger D. Gunfighters, Highwaymen & Vigilantes: Violence on the Frontier. University of California Press (March 23, 1987). pp. 99- 100. ISBN 978-0520060265.

Dworkin, Mark. "Charlie Siringo, Letter Writer". Western Outlaw Lawman Association Journal. Winter 2003, Vol. XI (4): 16–18.

Gatto, Steve. "Wyatt Earp History Page". WyattEarp.Net. Douglas Linder (2005). "Testimony of Virgil Earp in the Preliminary Hearing in the Earp Case". Famous Trials: The O. K. Corral Trial.

Wilkinson, Darryl (1992-07-22). "Johnny Ringo Called Gallatin Home as a Boy". Gallatin North Missourian.

Metz, Leon Claire. 1979. Dallas Stoudenmire: El Paso Marshal. Norman, University of Oklahoma Press. 162 p.

Cunningham, Sharon. – "The Allison Clan – A Visit"' "Butch Cassidy and Sundance Kid". Wyoming Tales and Trails. Barra, Allen (2008). Inventing Wyatt Earp: His Life and Many Legends. Lincoln, Nebraska: University of Nebraska Press. p. 440. ISBN 978-0-8032-2058-4. p.117

Carlson, Chip (2001). Tom Horn: Blood on the Moon: Dark History of the Murderous Cattle Detective. High

Plains Press. pp. 22–28. ISBN 978-0-931271-58-8.

Woog, Adam (February 28, 2010). Wyatt Earp. Chelsea House Publications. ISBN 1-60413-597-2. p.31

Nolan, Frederick (2009) [March 1992]. The Lincoln County War: A Documentary History (Revised ed.). Santa Fe, NM: Sunstone Presse. pp. 510, 219. ISBN 978-0-86534-721-2.

Taffin, John (2005). The Gun Digest Book of Cowboy Action Shooting: Guns · Gear · Tactics. Gun Digest Books. p. 256. ISBN 978-0-89689-140-1.

Funakoshi, Gichin (2001). Karate Jutsu: The Original Teachings of Master Funakoshi, translated by John Teramoto. Kodansha International Ltd. ISBN 4-7700-2681-1

Funakoshi, Gichin (1981). Karate-Do: My Way of Life, Kodansha International Ltd. ISBN 0-87011-463-8.

"GichinFunakoshi.com".

"Deconstructing Funakoshi".

John Stevens (1995). "Three Budo Masters: Kano, Funakoshi, Ueshiba". Kodansha International ISBN 4-7700-1852-5

"The Official Homepage of Nihon Karate-do Shotokai".

Funakoshi, Gichin (1975). The Twenty Guiding Principles of Karate: The Spiritual Legacy of the Master, translated by John Teramoto. Kodansha International Ltd. ISBN 4-7700-2796-6.

"Kosugi Hoan Shotokan Tiger".

Cook, Harry (2001). Shotokan Karate: A Precise History. England: Cook. Crawford, Roman Republican

Coinage, pp. 455, 456.

Taagepera, Rein (1979). "Size and Duration of Empires: Growth–Decline Curves, 600 BC to 600 AD". Social Science History. 3 (3/4): 115–138 [125]. doi:10.2307/1170959. JSTOR 1170959.

Cornell, The beginnings of Rome, pp. 215-218

Dionysius, iv. 64–85.[1]

Livy, i. 57-60

Cornell, Beginnings of Rome, pp. 226 - 228.

Aristotle, Politics, 5.1311a.

Cornell, Beginnings of Rome, pp. 215-218, 377, 378.

Drummond, Cambridge Ancient History, VII, part 2, p. 178.

Cornell, Beginnings of Rome, pp. 215-217.

Grant, The History of Rome, p. 33

Florus, Epitome, i. 11-12.

Grant, The History of Rome, pp. 37-41.

Pennell, Ancient Rome, Ch. II

Cornell, Beginnings of Rome, pp. 289-291.

Cornell, Beginnings of Rome, pp. 256-259

Orlin, A Companion to Roman Religion, pp. 59-60.

Beginnings of Rome, pp. 215-218, 256-261, 266.

Violence in Republican Rome, Oxford University Press, 1999, pp. 92–101.

Florus, Epitome, i. 13.

Grant, The History of Rome, pp. 48-49.

Grant, The History of Rome, p. 52.

Grant, The History of Rome, p. 53.

Cornell, Cambridge Ancient History, vol. 7-2, p. 338.

Livy, vi. 11, 13-30.

Cornell, Cambridge Ancient History, vol. 7-2, pp. 331, 332.

Cornell, Cambridge Ancient History, vol. 7-2, p. 337. Cornell explains that Livy confused the contents of the Lex Licinia Sextia of 366 the Lex Genucia of 342.

Livy, vi. 36-42.

Broughton, vol. I, pp. 108-114.

Brennan, The Praetorship, pp. 59-67

Brennan, The Praetorship, pp. 65-67

Cornell, Cambridge Ancient History, vol. 7-2, pp. 342, 343.

Brennan, The Praetorship, pp. 68, 69.

Cornell, Cambridge Ancient History, vol. 7-2, pp. 393, 394. Cornell gives an earlier date, before 318.

Humm, Appius Claudius Caecus, pp. 185-226.

Taylor, Voting Districts, pp. 132-138.

Bruce MacBain, "Appius Claudius Caecus and the Via Appia", in The Classical Quarterly, New Series, Vol. 30, No. 2 (1980), pp. 356-372.

Cornell, Cambridge Ancient History, vol. 7-2, p. 343.

Graham Maddox, "The Economic Causes of the Lex Hortensia", in Latomus, T. 42, Fasc. 2 (Apr.-Jun. 1983), pp. 277-286.

R. Develin, "'Provocatio" and Plebiscites'. Early Roman Legislation and the Historical Tradition", in Mnemosyne, Fourth Series, Vol. 31, Fasc. 1 (1978), pp. 45-60.

Cornell, Cambridge Ancient History, vol. 7-2, pp. 340,

341.

Cornell, The Beginnings of Rome, p. 342

Franke, Cambridge Ancient History, vol. 7, part 2, p. 484.

Grant, The History of Rome, p. 78.

Dionysius of Halicarnassus, xix. 5, 6.

Plutarch, Pyrrhus, 14.

Franke, Cambridge Ancient History, vol. 7, part 2, pp. 456, 457.

Cicero, Cato Maior de Senectute, 6.

Plutarch, Pyrrhus, 18, 19.

Franke, Cambridge Ancient History, vol. 7, part 2, pp. 466-471.

Dionysius of Halicarnassus, xx. 3.

Plutarch, Pyrrhus, 21 § 9.

Cassius Dio, x. 5.

Franke, Cambridge Ancient History, vol. 7, part 2, pp. 473-480.

Grant, The History of Rome, p. 80

Scullard, Cambridge Ancient History, vol. 7, part 2, pp. 517-537.

Goldsworthy, The Punic Wars, p. 88.

Scullard, Cambridge Ancient History, vol. 7, part 2, pp. 554-557.

Crawford, Roman Republican Coinage, pp. 292, 293.

Scullard, Cambridge Ancient History, vol. 7, part 2, pp. 559-564.

Scullard, Cambridge Ancient History, vol. 7, part 2, pp. 565-569.

Hoyos, Companion to the Punic Wars

Scullard, Cambridge Ancient History, pp. 28-31.

Hoyos, Companion to the Punic Wars, pp. 216-219.

Scullard, Cambridge Ancient History, pp. 33-36.

Scullard, Cambridge Ancient History, p. 37

Scullard, Cambridge Ancient History, p. 39.

Briscoe, Cambridge Ancient History, p. 46.

Fronda, Companion to the Punic Wars, pp. 251, 252.

Briscoe, Cambridge Ancient History, p. 47.

Livy, xxi. 38

Briscoe, Cambridge Ancient History, p. 48.

Polybius (iii. 117) gives 70,000 dead. Livy (xxii. 49) gives 47,700 dead and 19,300 prisoners.

Sylloge Nummorum Graecorum, Great Britain, Volume IX, British Museum, Part 2: Spain, London, 2002, n° 102.

Briscoe, Cambridge Ancient History

Matyszak, The Enemies of Rome, p. 47

Grant, The History of Rome, p. 115

Eckstein, Rome Enters the Greek East, p. 42.

Eckstein, Arthur. "Rome Enters the Greek East". p43

Matyszak, The Enemies of Rome, p. 49

Grant, The History of Rome, p. 117

Eckstein, Arthur. "Rome Enters the Greek East"

Grant, The History of Rome, p. 119

Eckstein, Arthur. "Rome Enters the Greek East". p52

Naples National Archaeological Museum (Inv. No. 5634).

Lane Fox, The Classical World, p. 326

Eckstein, Arthur. "Rome Enters the Greek East". p55

Grant, The History of Rome, p. 120

Goldsworthy, In the Name of Rome

Matyszak, The Enemies of Rome, p. 53

History of Rome – The republic, Isaac Asimov.

Pennell, Ancient Rome, Ch. XV, para. 24

Goldsworthy, The Punic Wars, p. 338

Goldsworthy, The Punic Wars, p. 339

Abbott, 96

Bishop, Paul. "Rome: Transition from Republic to Empire" (PDF). Hillsborough Community College

Stobart, J.C. (1978). "III". In Maguinness, W.S; Scullard, H.H. The Grandeur That was Rome (4th ed.)

Santosuosso, Storming the Heavens, p. 29

Sallust, The Jugurthine War, XII

Matyszak, The Enemies of Rome, p. 64

Crawford, Roman Republican Coinage, pp. 449-451.

Matyszak, The Enemies of Rome, p. 77

Appian, Civil Wars, 1, 117

Santosuosso, Storming the Heavens, p. 43

Florus, The Epitome of Roman history, Book 3, ch. 5

Matyszak, The Enemies of Rome, p. 76

Grant, The History of Rome, p. 158

Lane Fox, The Classical World, p. 363

Plutarch, Lives, Pompey

Florus, The Epitome of Roman history, Book 3, ch. 6

Roller, Duane W. (2010). Cleopatra: a biography. Oxford: Oxford University Press. ISBN 9780195365535, p. 175.

Walker, Susan. "Cleopatra in Pompeii?" in Papers of the British School at Rome, 76 (2008): 35–46 and 345-8

Goldsworthy, In the Name of Rome, p. 237

Luttwak, The Grand Strategy of the Roman Empire, p. 7

Boak, A History of Rome to 565 A.D., p. 87

Santosuosso, Storming the Heavens, p. 18

Webster, The Roman Imperial Army, p. 156

Smith, Service in the Post-Marian Roman Army, p. 2

Gabba, Republican Rome, The Army and The Allies, p. 9

Santosuosso, Storming the Heavens, p. 11

Webster, The Roman Imperial Army, p. 143

Santosuosso, Storming the Heavens, p. 10

Gabba, Republican Rome, The Army And the Allies, p. 1

Gabba, Republican Rome, The Army and The Allies, p. 25

Luttwak, The Grand Strategy of the Roman Empire, p. 14

Webster, The Roman Imperial Army, p. 116

Luttwak, The Grand Strategy of the Roman Empire, p. 15

Luttwak, The Grand Strategy of the Roman Empire, p. 43

Tacitus. Annales. II.49.

D.B. Saddington (2011) [2007]. "the Evolution of the Roman Imperial Fleets," in Paul Erdkamp (ed), A Companion to the Roman Army, 201–217. Malden,

Oxford, Chichester: Wiley-Blackwell. ISBN 978-1-4051-2153-8. Plate 12.2 on p. 204.

Coarelli, Filippo (1987), I Santuari del Lazio in età repubblicana. NIS, Rome, pp 35–84.

Cornell, Beginnings of Rome, pp. 215-216.

Thomas A.J. McGinn, Prostitution, Sexuality and the Law in Ancient Rome (Oxford University Press, 1998), p. 65ff.

Drummond, Cambridge Ancient History, vol. 7, part 2, p. 126.

Alföldy, Geza, The Social History of Rome, p. 17.

Cornell, Beginnings of Rome, pp. 288-291.

Flower, Cambridge Companion to the Roman Republic, pp. 173-175

D'Arms, J. B., "Senators' Involvement in Commerce in the Late Republic: Some Ciceronian Evidence", Memoirs of the American Academy in Rome, Vol. 36, The Seaborne Commerce of Ancient Rome: Studies in Archaeology and History (1980), pp. 77-89, University of Michigan Press for the American Academy in Rome.

David Johnston, Roman Law in Context (Cambridge University Press, 1999), pp. 33-34.

Bruce W. Frier and Thomas A.J. McGinn, A Casebook on Roman Family Law (Oxford University Press, 2004), pp. 20, 53, 54

Cornell, Beginnings of Rome, pp. 265-268, 283.

Bannon, Gardens and Neighbors, pp. 5–10.

Drummond, Cambridge Ancient History, vol. 7, part 2, pp. 118-122, 135, 136.

Cornell, Beginnings of Rome, pp. 265-268.

Gabba, Cambridge Ancient History, vol. 8, pp. 197-198.

Lintott, Cambridge Ancient History, vol. 9, p. 55

Cornell, Beginnings of Rome, pp. 328-329.

Bannon, Gardens and Neighbors, pp. 5–10; citing Hodge, Roman Aqueducts, p. 219 for Cato's diatribe against the misuse of aqueduct water by L. Furius Purpureus, consul in 196.

Nicolet, Cambridge Ancient History, vol. 9, p. 619.

Rosenstein, Nathan, "Aristocrats and Agriculture in the Middle Republic", The Journal of Roman Studies, Vol. 98 (2008), pp. 2-16.

Nicolet, Cambridge Ancient History, vol. 9, pp. 612-615

Drummond, Cambridge Ancient History, vol. 7, part 2, pp. 118-122.

Gabba, Cambridge Ancient History, vol. 8, pp. 237-239.

Drummond, Cambridge Ancient History, vol. 7, part 2, pp. 118-122.

Fowler, W. Warde (1899). Roman Festivals of the Period of the Republic. Port Washington, NY: Kennikat Press. pp. 202–204.

Rüpke, Companion to Roman Religion, p. 4.

Beard, North, Price, Religions of Rome, Vol. I, pp. 30-35.

Robert Schilling, "The Decline and Survival of Roman Religion", Roman and European Mythologies University of Chicago Press, 1992, p. 115

Halm, Companion to Roman Religion, pp. 241, 242.

Rüpke, Companion to Roman Religion, p. 5.

Erich S. Gruen, Erich S., "The Bacchanalia affair", in Studies in Greek Culture and Roman Policy, University of California Press, 1996, p. 34 ff.

Rosenberger, Companion to Roman Religion, pp. 295-298; Livy, xxvii. 37, cited by Halm, Companion to Roman Religion, p. 244; see also Rosenberger, p. 297.

Cornell, The beginnings of Rome, p. 264.

Barbette Stanley Spaeth, "The Goddess Ceres and the Death of Tiberius Gracchus", Historia: Zeitschrift für Alte Geschichte, Vol. 39, No. 2 (1990), pp. 185-186.

Lott, John. B., The Neighborhoods of Augustan Rome, Cambridge, Cambridge University Press, 2004, ISBN 0-521-82827-9, pp. 31, 35, citing Cato, On agriculture, 5.3., and Dionysius of Halicarnassus, 4.14.2-4 (excerpt), Trans. Cary, Loeb, Cambridge, 1939.

Ovid, Fasti, v, 129-145

Crawford, Roman Republican Coinage, p. 312.

Cornell, The beginnings of Rome, p. 342

Lipka, M., Roman Gods: a conceptual approach, Versnel, H., S., Frankfurter, D., Hahn, J., (Editors), Religions in the Graeco-Roman world, BRILL, 2009, pp. 171-172

Rosenberger, Companion to Roman Religion, p. 299.

Cunham, Cambridge Companion to the Roman Republic, p. 155.

Beard, Mary, "The Sexual Status of Vestal Virgins," The Journal of Roman Studies, Vol. 70, (1980), pp. 12-27; and Parker, Holt N. "Why Were the Vestals Virgins?

Or the Chastity of Women and the Safety of the Roman State", American Journal of Philology, Vol. 125, No. 4. (2004), pp. 563–601.

Cornell, Beginnings of Rome, p. 264.

Orlin, Eric M., Foreign Cults in Republican Rome: Rethinking the Pomerial Rule, Memoirs of the American Academy in Rome, Vol. 47 (2002), pp. 4-5.

Roller, Lynn Emrich (1999). In Search of God the Mother: The Cult of Anatolian Cybele, Berkeley and Los Angeles, California: University of California Press, pp. 282 - 285. ISBN 0-520-21024-7

Crawford, Roman Republican Coinage, pp. 487-495.

Orlin, Companion to Roman Religion, p. 58.

Beard, North, Price, Religions of Rome, Vol. I, pp. 44, 59, 60, 143.

Eden, P.T., "Venus and the Cabbage" Hermes, 91, (1963) p. 456.

Schilling, R. La Religion romaine de Venus, BEFAR, Paris, 1954, p.87

Brouwer, Henrik H. J., Bona Dea, The Sources and a Gargarin, M. and Fantham, E. (editors). The Oxford Encyclopedia of Ancient Greece and Rome, Volume 1. p. 145.

The Economic History Review, New Series, Vol. 53, No. 1. (February, 2000), pp. 29–59 (39)

Ceccarelli, L., in Bell, S., and Carpino, A., A, (Editors) A Companion to the Etruscans (Blackwell Companions to the Ancient World), Blackwell Publishing, 2016, p. 33

Astin, Rawson, Morel, Cambridge Ancient History, vol. 9, pp. 181-185, 439, 453, 495.

Bradley, Mark, Colour and Meaning in Ancient Rome, Cambridge Classical Studies, Cambridge University Press, 2011, pp. 189, 194-195

Edmondson, Roman Dress and the Fabrics of Roman Culture, pp. 28-30; Keith, p. 200.

Sebesta, The World of Roman Costume, pp. 54-56.

Vout, Caroline, "The Myth of the Toga: Understanding the History of Roman Dress", Greece & Rome, 43, No. 2 (Oct., 1996), pp. 211, 212.

Edmondson, Roman Dress and the Fabrics of Roman Culture, p. 33.

Sebesta, The World of Roman Costume, p. 70, citing Columella, 12, praef. 9-10, 12.3.6.

Cato, De Agri Cultura ch. 74-90, 104-125, 156-157, 158-162.

Nanette R. Pacal, "The Legacy of Roman Education (in the Forum)", in The Classical Journal, Vol. 79, No. 4. (April – May 1984)

Oxford Classical Dictionary, Edited by Simon Hornblower and Antony Spawforth, Third Edition. Oxford; New York: Oxford University Press, 1996

Joseph Farrell, Latin Language and Latin Culture (Cambridge University Press, 2001), pp. 74–75; Richard A. Bauman, Women and Politics in Ancient Rome (Routledge, 1992, 1994), pp. 51–52.

Toynbee, J. M. C. (December 1971). "Roman Art". The Classical Review. 21 (3): 439–442.

doi:10.1017/S0009840X00221331. JSTOR 708631.

Austin, Roland G. "Roman Board Games. I", Greece & Rome 4:10, October 1934. pp. 24–34. Keen, Maurice Hugh (2005). Chivalry. Yale University Press. p. 44. ISBN 9780300107678. | access-date= requires | url= (help)

HOLT Literature & Language Arts. Houston, Texas: Holt, Rinehart, and Winston. 2003. pp. 100–101. ISBN 0-03-056498-0.

Keen, Maurice Hugh (2005). Chivalry. Yale University Press. p. 102.

Gautier (1891), p. 2

Flori (1998)

Dougherty, Martin (2008). Weapons and Fighting Techniques of the Medieval Warrior 1000 - 1500 AD. Chartwell Books. p. 74. ISBN 9780785834250.

Huizinga (1924), p. 28

Hoad (1993), p. 74

"Definition of CHIVALRY". www.merriam-webster.com. Daniel Eisenberg, A Study of Don Quixote, Newark, Delaware, Juan de la Cuesta, 1987, ISBN 0936388315, pp. 205-223: "The Influence of Don Quixote on the Romantic Movement".

Daniel Eisenberg, A Study of "Don Quixote", Newark, Delaware, Juan de la Cuesta, 1987,ISBN 0936388315, p. 148.

"Origin of the Knights". Knights of Chivalry. Retrieved 2018-02-28.

Historical View of the Literatures of the South of

Europe, trans. Thomas Roscoe, 4th edition, London, 1885-88, Vol. I, pp. 76-77.

Keen (2005), p. 42

Holt. Holt Literature and Language Arts Course Six. Houston. TX. p. 100. ISBN 0030564980.

Sweeney (1983)

Corrêa de Oliveira (1993), p. 10

Keen (2005), p. 56

Keen (2005), p. 62

"The Life of St. Gerald, by Odo". Penn State Press. 1954. p. 371.

Chivalry, Brittanica Encyclopedia

Keen (2005), pp. 44–45

Bromiley (1994), p. 272

Tucker (1987), p. 168

Huizinga (1924), p. "Pessimism and the ideal of the sublime life": 30

Gravett (2008), p. 267

Wilkins (2010), p. 168

Nordheimer, Jon (January 18, 1985). "Bombing Case Offers a Stark Look at Abortion Conflicts". The New York Times. p. 12.

Beers, Paul G. (Fall 1994). "The Wythe County Lynching of Raymond Bird: Progressivism vs. Mob Violence in the '20s". Appalachian Journal. 22 (1). p. 38.

 Frost, Stanley (1924). The Challenge of the Klan. reprint New York, 1969. p. 68.

The Birkenhead Drill by Doug Phillips

Oakeshott (1980), p. 255

Felson (2002)

Walker, Colin (2007). Brownsea:B-P's Acorn, The World's First Scout Camp. Write Books. ISBN 1-905546-21-1.

Manchester (1978)

"American Rhetoric: General Douglas MacArthur -- Sylvanus Thayer Award Address (Duty, Honor, Country)". americanrhetoric.com.

Daniel Eisenberg, A Study of "Don Quixote", Newark, Delaware, Juan de la Cuesta,1987, ISBN 0936388315, pp. 41-77, revised Spanish translation in Biblioteca Virtual Cervantes.

Avalon to Camelot, vol. 2, No. 2 (1986 [1987]), p. 2., Bromiley, Geoffrey W. (1994). International Standard Bible Corrêa de Oliveira, Plinio (1993). Nobility and Analogous Traditional Elites in the Allocutions of Pius XII. ISBN 0-8191-9310-0.

Crouch, David (2005). The Birth of Nobility: Constructing Aristocracy in England and France 900–1300. Harlow, UK: Pearson. ISBN 0-582-36981-9.

Felson, Richard B. (2002). "Violence and gender reexamined". Law and public policy. Washington, DC: American Psychological Association. pp. 67–82.

Flori, Jean (1998). La Chevalerie. J. P. Gisserot. ISBN 2877473457.

Gautier, Léon (1891). Chivalry. translated by Henry Frith.

Gravett, Christopher (2008). Knight: Noble Warrior of England 1200–1600. Oxford: Osprey Publishing.

Hoad, T. F. Hoad (1993). The Concise Oxford Dictionary of English Etymology. Oxford University Press.

Hodges, Kenneth (2005). Forging Chivalric Communities in Malory's Le Morte Darthur. New York: Palgrave Macmillan.

Huizinga, Johan (1924) [1919]. The Autumn of the Middle Ages.

Keen, Maurice Keen (2005). Chivalry. New Haven, CT: Yale University Press.

Manchester, William R. (1978). American Caesar: Douglas MacArthur 1880-1964. Boston & Toronto: Little, Brown and Company.

Oakeshott, R. E. (1980). European Weapons and Armour: from the Renaissance to the Industrial Revolution.

Sweeney, James Ross (1983). "Chivalry". Dictionary of the Middle Ages. III

Tucker, Ruth (1987). Daughters of the Church. ISBN 0-310-45741-6.

Wilkins, Christopher (2010). The Last Knight Errant: Sir Edward Woodville and the Age of Chivalry. London & New York: I. B. Tauris. Brink, Stefan (2008). "Who were the Vikings?". In Brink, Stefan; Price, Neil. The Viking World. Routledge. pp. 4–10. ISBN 978-0415692625.

Brookes, Ian (2004). Chambers concise dictionary. Allied Publishers. ISBN 9788186062364.

D'Amato, Raffaele (2010). The Varangian Guard 988–

453. Osprey Publishing. ISBN 978-1-84908-179-5.

Derry, T.K. (2012). A History of Scandinavia: Norway, Sweden, Denmark, Finland, Iceland. London and Minneapolis: University of Minnesota Press. ISBN 978-0-81663-799-7.

Educational Company of Ireland (10 October 2000). Irish-English/English-Irish Easy Reference Dictionary. Roberts Rinehart. ISBN 978-1-4616-6031-6.

Fitzhugh, William W.; Ward, Elisabeth I. (2000). Vikings: The North Atlantic Saga; (an Exhibition at the National Museum of Natural History, Smithsonian Institution, Washington D.C., April 29, 2000 – September 5, 2000). Washington: Smithsonian Institution Press. ISBN 978-1560989707.

Hall, Richard Andrew (2007). The World of the Vikings. Thames & Hudson. ISBN 978-0500051443.

Hall, Richard (January 1990). Viking Age Archaeology in Britain and Ireland. Shire. ISBN 978-0747800637.

Lindqvist, Thomas (4 September 2003). "Early Political Organisation: (a) An Introductory Survey". In Helle, Knut. The Cambridge History of Scandinavia: Prehistory to 1520. Cambridge University Press. pp. 160–67. ISBN 978-0521472999.

Roesdahl, Else (1998). The Vikings. Penguin Books. ISBN 978-0140252828.

Sawyer, Peter Hayes (1 February 1972). Age of the Vikings. Palgrave Macmillan. ISBN 978-0312013653.

Sawyer, Peter, ed. (1997). The Oxford Illustrated History of the Vikings. Oxford, UK: Oxford University

Press. ISBN 978-0-19-820526-5.

Williams, Gareth (2007). "Kingship, Christianity and coinage: monetary and political perspectives on silver economy in the Viking Age". In Graham-Campbell, James; Williams, Gareth. Silver Economy in the Viking Age. Left Coast Press. pp. 177–214. ISBN 978-1598742220.

Wolf, Kirsten (1 January 2004). Daily Life of the Vikings. Greenwood Publishing Group. ISBN 978-0-313-32269-3. Ikeuchi Hiroshi. "Shiragi no karō ni tsuite." Tōyō-gakuhō 24.1 (1936), pp. 1–34

Joe, Wanna J. and Hongkyu A. Choe. Traditional Korea, A Cultural History. Seoul: Hollym, 1997.

Lee, Ki-dong. "The Silla Society and Hwarang Corps." Journal of Social Sciences and Humanities, 65 (June 1987):1-16

Lee, Peter H. (trans.) Lives of Eminent Korean Monks: The Haedong Kosŭng Chŏn (by Gakhun). Cambridge, MA: Harvard University Press, 1969.

McBride, Richard D., II. "The Hwarang segi Manuscripts: An In-Progress Colonial Period Fiction." Korea Journal, vol. 45, no. 3 (Autumn 2005):230-260.[1]

McBride, Richard D., II. "Silla Buddhism and the Hwarang." Korean Studies 34 (2010): 54-89.

Mohan, Pankaj N. "Maitreya Cult in Early Shilla: Focusing on Hwarang in Maitreya-Dynasty." Seoul Journal of Korean Studies, 14 (2001):149-174.

Rutt, Richard. "The Flower Boys of Silla (Hwarang), Notes on the Sources." Transactions of the Korea

Branch of the Royal Asiatic Society, 38 (October 1961):1-66.

Tikhonov, Vladimir. "Hwarang Organization: Its Functions and Ethics." Korea Journal, vol. 38, no. 2 (Summer 1998):318-338. [2]

Waley, A. "The Book of Songs" London, 1937.

McBride II, R. (n.d.). Retrieved 6 December 2014, from Silla Buddhism and the Hwarang segi Manuscripts. Korean Studies. (2007) Vol. 31 Issue 1, 19-38. 20p

McBride II, R. (n.d.). Retrieved 6 December 2014, from Silla Buddhism and the Hwarang. Korean Studies. Vol. 34 Issue 1. (2010) 54-89. 36p

ACTA Black Belt Manual,. (2007). History of Tae Kwon Do. Retrieved 6 December 2014, from ACTA Black Belt Manual

Hwarangkwan.org,. (2014). Kwan_Chang. Retrieved 6 December 2014, from http://www.hwarangkwan.org/kwan_chang.htm

Shin, Chi-Yun. "Glossary of key terms". New York: New York University Press, 2005. "Modern Army Combatives - History". Archived from the original on June 28, 2010.

Filipino Kali is Alive and Well in Today's Police and Military Training Jim Wagner, USA Dojo.com

'Crafty Dog' teaches knife, stick fighting Michael Heckman, Fort Hood Sentinel, August 6, 2009. Marc "Crafty Dog" Denny from the Dog Brothers helped Matt Larsen develop fighting methods taught in the Modern Army Combatives Program

Jessica Zafra. "The Greatest Filipino Export is Kicking Ass". Philippine Star.

Ross Harper Alonso. "In the Stick of Things". Philippine Daily Inquirer. Archived from the original on 2010-06-15.

"The Bladed Hand: The Global Impact of Filipino Martial Arts trailer" Matthews, Warren (2010). World Religions. Belmont, CA: Cengage Learning. p. 199. ISBN 9780495603856.

Nitobe, Inazo (2010). Bushido, The Soul of Japan. Kodansha International. p. 81. ISBN 9784770050113.

"The Zen of Japanese Nationalism", by Robert H. Shart, in Curators of the Buddha, edited by Donald Lopez, p. 111

"Tokugawa shogunate"

Willcock, Hiroko (2008). The Japanese Political Thought of Uchimura Kanzō (1861-1930): Synthesizing Bushidō, Christianity, Nationalism, and Liberalism. Edwin Mellen Press. ISBN 077345151X. Koyo gunkan is the earliest comprehensive extant work that provides a notion of Bushido as a samurai ethos and the value system of the samurai tradition.

Ikegami, Eiko, The Taming of the Samurai, Harvard University Press, 1995. p. 278

Kasaya, Kazuhiko (2014). 武士道 第一章 武士道という語の登場 [Bushido Chapter I Appearance of the word Bushido] (in Japanese). NTT publishing. p. 7. ISBN 4757143222.

Friday, Karl F. "Bushidō or Bull? A Medieval

Historian's Perspective on the Imperial Army and the Japanese Warrior Tradition". The History Teacher, Vol. 27, No. 3 (May 1994), pp. 340.

Nitobe, Inazō (1899). Bushidō: The soul of Japan.

Arthur May Knapp (1896). "Feudal and Modern Japan". Retrieved 2010-01-02.

"The Zen of Japanese Nationalism," by Robert H. Sharf, in Curators of the Buddha, edited by Donald Lopez, p. 111

"Onna-Bugeisha – The Female Samurai". Foreign policy. 2018-05-24. Retrieved 2018-08-30.

Shimabukuro, Masayuki; Pellman, Leonard (2007). Flashing Steel: Mastering Eishin-Ryu Swordsmanship, 2nd edition. Berkeley, CA: Blue Snake Books. p. 2. ISBN 9781583941973.

William Scott Wilson, Ideals of the Samurai: Writings of Japanese Warriors (Kodansha, 1982) ISBN 0-89750-081-4

"The Samurai Series: The Book of Five Rings, Hagakure -The Way of the Samurai & Bushido - The Soul of Japan" ELPN Press (November, 2006) ISBN 1-934255-01-7

Meirion and Susie Harries, Soldiers of the Sun: The Rise and Fall of the Imperial Japanese Army p 7 ISBN 0-394-56935-0

Eiko Ikegami. The Taming of the Samurai: Honorific Individualism and the Making of Modern Japan. Cambridge, MA: Harvard University Press, 1995.

Karl Friday. Bushidō or Bull? A Medieval Historian's

Perspective on the Imperial Army and the Japanese Warrior Tradition. The History Teacher, Volume 27, Number 3, May 1994, pages 339-349.[1]

Oleg Benesch. Inventing the Way of the Samurai: Nationalism, Internationalism, and Bushido in Modern Japan. Oxford: Oxford University Press, 2014. ISBN 0198706626, ISBN 9780198706625

Herbert P. Bix, Hirohito and the Making of Modern Japan p 42-3 ISBN 0-06-019314-X

"No Surrender: Background History"

David Powers, "Japan: No Surrender in World War Two"

John W. Dower, War Without Mercy: Race & Power in the Pacific War p1 ISBN 0-394-50030-X

Richard Overy, Why the Allies Won p 6 ISBN 0-393-03925-0

Edwin P. Hoyt, Japan's War, p 334 ISBN 0-07-030612-5

John Toland, The Rising Sun: The Decline and Fall of the Japanese Empire 1936-1945 p 444 Random House New York 1970

John Toland, The Rising Sun: The Decline and Fall of the Japanese Empire 1936-1945 p 539 Random House New York 1970

Edwin P. Hoyt, Japan's War, p 356 ISBN 0-07-030612-5

Edwin P. Hoyt, Japan's War, p 360 ISBN 0-07-030612-5

Edwin P. Hoyt, Japan's War, p 256 ISBN 0-07-030612-5

Edwin P. Hoyt, Japan's War, p 257 ISBN 0-07-030612-5

"Bushido | Japanese history". Encyclopedia Britannica. Retrieved 2017-08-21.

"ospreysamurai.com". www.ospreysamurai.com.

Cleary, Thomas Training the Samurai Mind: A Bushido Sourcebook Shambhala (May 2008) ISBN 1-59030-572-8

Mikiso Hane Modern Japan: A Historical Survey, Third Edition Westview Press (January 2001) ISBN 0-8133-3756-9

Zeami Motokiyo "Atsumori"

Bushido: The Soul of Japan

"Monumenta Nipponica". Archived from the original on 2008-02-15. Birley, Marcus Aurelius, 229–30. The thesis of single authorship was first proposed in H. Dessau's "Über Zeit und Persönlichkeit der Scriptoes Historiae Augustae" (in German), Hermes 24 (1889), 337ff.

Birley, Marcus Aurelius, 230. On the HA Verus, see Barnes, 65–74.

Beard; Birley, Marcus Aurelius, 226.

Birley, Marcus Aurelius, 227.

Birley, Marcus Aurelius, 228–29, 253.

Birley, Marcus Aurelius, 227–28.

Birley, Marcus Aurelius, 228.

Magill, Frank Northen (2003-01-23). Dictionary of World Biography. ISBN 9781579580407.

Historia MA I.9–10

Van Ackeren, 139.

Birley, Marcus Aurelius, 33.

Dio 69.21.1; HA Marcus 1.10; McLynn, Marcus Aurelius: Warrior, Philosopher, Emperor, 24.

Dio 69.21.1; HA Marcus 1.9; McLynn, Marcus
Aurelius: Warrior, Philosopher, Emperor, 24.

Van Ackeren, 78.

Dean, 32.

Birley, Marcus Aurelius, 49.

HA Marcus 1.2, 1.4; Birley, Marcus Aurelius, 28;
McLynn, 14.

Dio 69.21.2, 71.35.2–3; Birley, Marcus Aurelius, 31.

Codex Inscriptionum Latinarum 14.3579 Archived 29
April 2012 at the Wayback Machine.; Birley, Marcus
Aurelius, 29; McLynn, 14, 575 n. 53, citing Ronald
Syme, Roman Papers 1.244.

Birley, Marcus Aurelius, 29; McLynn, Marcus
Aurelius: Warrior, Philosopher, Emperor, 14.

Birley, Marcus Aurelius, 29, citing Pliny, Epistulae
8.18.

Birley, Marcus Aurelius, 30.

Birley, Marcus Aurelius, 31, 44.

Birley, Marcus Aurelius, 31.

Farquharson, 1.95–96.

Meditations 1.1, qtd. and tr. Birley, Marcus Aurelius,
31.

HA Marcus 2.1 and Meditations 5.4, qtd. in Birley,
Marcus Aurelius, 32.

Meditations 1.3, qtd. in Birley, Marcus Aurelius, 35.

Meditations 1.17.7, qtd. and tr. Birley, Marcus
Aurelius, 35.

Ad Marcum Caesarem 2.8.2 (= Haines 1.142), qtd. and
tr. Birley, Marcus Aurelius, 31.

Birley, Marcus Aurelius, 31–32.

Meditations 1.1, qtd. and tr. Birley, Marcus Aurelius, 35.

Birley, Marcus Aurelius, 35.

Meditations 1.17.2; Farquharson, 1.102; McLynn, Marcus Aurelius: Warrior, Philosopher, Emperor, 23; cf. Meditations 1.17.11; Farquharson, 1.103.

McLynn, Marcus Aurelius: Warrior, Philosopher, Emperor, 20–21.

Meditations 1.4; McLynn, Marcus Aurelius: Warrior, Philosopher, Emperor, 20.

HA Marcus 2.2, 4.9; Meditations 1.3; Birley, Marcus Aurelius, 37; McLynn, Marcus Aurelius: Warrior, Philosopher, Emperor, 21–22.

HA Marcus 2.6; Birley, Marcus Aurelius, 38; McLynn, Marcus Aurelius: Warrior, Philosopher, Emperor, 21.

Birley, Lives of the Later Caesars, 109, 109 n.8; Marcus Aurelius, 40, 270 n.27, citing Bonner Historia-Augusta Colloquia 1966/7, 39ff.

HA Marcus 2.3; Birley, Marcus Aurelius, 40, 270 n.27.

Birley, Marcus Aurelius, 40, citing Aelius Aristides, Oratio 32 K; McLynn, Marcus Aurelius: Warrior, Philosopher, Emperor, 21.

Meditations 1.10; Birley, Marcus Aurelius, 40; McLynn, Marcus Aurelius: Warrior, Philosopher, Emperor, 22.

Birley, Marcus Aurelius, 40, 270 n.28, citing A.S.L. Farquharson, The Meditations of Marcus Antoninus (Oxford, 1944) 2.453.

Portrait of the Emperor Marcus Aurelius.

Birley, Marcus Aurelius, 41–42.

HA Hadrian 23.10, qtd. in Birley, Marcus Aurelius, 42.

Birley, Marcus Aurelius, 42. Van Ackeren, 142. On the succession to Hadrian, see also: T.D. Barnes, "Hadrian and Lucius Verus", Journal of Roman Studies 57:1-2 (1967): 65–79; J. VanderLeest, "Hadrian, Lucius Verus, and the Arco di Portogallo", Phoenix 49:4 (1995): 319–30.

HA Aelius 6.2-3

HA Hadrian 23.15–16; Birley, Marcus Aurelius, 45; "Hadrian to the Antonines", 148.

Dio 69.17.1; HA Aelius 3.7, 4.6, 6.1–7; Birley, "Hadrian to the Antonines", 147.

Birley, Marcus Aurelius, 46. Date: Birley, "Hadrian to the Antonines", 148.

Weigel.

Dio 69.21.1; HA Hadrian 24.1; HA Aelius 6.9; HA Antoninus Pius 4.6–7; Birley, Marcus Aurelius, 48–49.

HA Marcus 5.3; Birley, Marcus Aurelius, 49.

Birley, Marcus Aurelius, 49–50.

HA Marcus 5.6–8, qtd. and tr. Birley, Marcus Aurelius, 50.

Birley, Marcus Aurelius, 80–81.

Dio 69.22.4; HA Hadrian 25.5–6; Birley, Marcus Aurelius, 50–51. Hadrian's suicide attempts: Dio 69.22.1–4; HA Hadrian 24.8–13.

HA Hadrian 25.7; Birley, Marcus Aurelius, 53.

HA Antoninus Pius 5.3, 6.3; Birley, Marcus Aurelius,

55–56; "Hadrian to the Antonines", 151.

Birley, Marcus Aurelius, 55; "Hadrian to the Antonines", 151.

HA Marcus 6.2; Verus 2.3–4; Birley, Marcus Aurelius, 53–54.

Dio 71.35.5; HA Marcus 6.3; Birley, Marcus Aurelius, 56.

Meditations 6.30, qtd. and tr. Birley, Marcus Aurelius, 57; cf. Marcus Aurelius, 270 n.9, with notes on the translation.

HA Marcus 6.3; Birley, Marcus Aurelius, 57.

Birley, Marcus Aurelius, 57, 272 n.10, citing Codex Inscriptionum Latinarum 6.32, 6.379, cf. Inscriptiones Latinae Selectae 360.

Meditations 5.16, qtd. and tr. Birley, Marcus Aurelius, 57.

Meditations 8.9, qtd. and tr. Birley, Marcus Aurelius, 57.

Birley, Marcus Aurelius, 57–58.

Ad Marcum Caesarem 4.7, qtd. and tr. Birley, Marcus Aurelius, 90.

HA Marcus 6.5; Birley, Marcus Aurelius, 58.

Birley, Marcus Aurelius, 89.

Ad Marcum Caesarem 5.1, qtd. and tr. Birley, Marcus Aurelius, 89.

Ad Marcum Caesarem 4.8, qtd. and tr. Birley, Marcus Aurelius, 89.

Dio 71.36.3; Birley, Marcus Aurelius, 89.

Birley, Marcus Aurelius, 90–91.

HA Antoninus Pius 10.2, qtd. and tr. Birley, Marcus Aurelius, 91.

Birley, Marcus Aurelius, 91.

Birley, Marcus Aurelius, 61.

HA Marcus 3.6; Birley, Marcus Aurelius, 62.

HA Marcus 2.4; Birley, Marcus Aurelius, 62.

Alan Cameron, review of Anthony Birley's Marcus Aurelius, Classical Review 17:3 (1967): 347.

Vita Sophistae 2.1.14; Birley, Marcus Aurelius, 63–64.

Aulus Gellius, Noctes Atticae 9.2.1–7; Birley, Marcus Aurelius, 64–65.

Aulus Gellius, Noctes Atticae 19.12, qtd. and tr. Birley, Marcus Aurelius, 65.

Birley, Marcus Aurelius, 65.

Birley, Marcus Aurelius, 67–68, citing Champlin, Fronto and Antonine Rome, esp. chs. 3 and 4.

Birley, Marcus Aurelius, 65–67.

Champlin, Fronto, 1–2.

Mellor, 460.

Cf., e.g.: Mellor, 461 and passim.

Birley, Marcus Aurelius, 69.

Ad Marcum Caesarem 4.6 (= Haines 1.80ff), qtd. and tr. Birley, Marcus Aurelius, 76.

Ad Marcum Caesarem 4.6 (= Haines 1.80ff); Birley, Marcus Aurelius, 76–77.

Ad Marcum Caesarem 3.10–11 (= Haines 1.50ff), qtd. and tr. Birley, Marcus Aurelius, 73.

Birley, Marcus Aurelius, 73.

Champlin, "Chronology of Fronto", 138.

Ad Marcum Caesarem 5.74 (=Haines 2.52ff), qtd. and tr. Birley, Marcus Aurelius, 73.

Birley, Marcus Aurelius, 77. On the date, see Champlin, "Chronology of Fronto", 142, who (with Bowersock, Greek Sophists in the Roman Empire (1964), 93ff) argues for a date in the 150s; Birley, Marcus Aurelius, 78–79, 273 n.17 (with Ameling, Herodes Atticus (1983), 1.61ff, 2.30ff) argues for 140.

Ad Marcum Caesarem 3.2 (= Haines 1.58ff), qtd. and tr. Birley, Marcus Aurelius, 77–78.

Ad Marcum Caesarem 3.3 (= Haines 1.62ff); Birley, Marcus Aurelius, 78.

Ad Marcum Caesarem 3.3 (= Haines 1.62ff), qtd. and tr. Birley, Marcus Aurelius, 79.

Birley, Marcus Aurelius, 80.

Ad Marcum Caesarem 4.13 (= Haines 1.214ff), qtd. and tr. Birley, Marcus Aurelius, 93.

Ad Marcum Caesarem 4.3.1 (= Haines 1.2ff); Birley, Marcus Aurelius, 94.

HA Marcus 3.5–8, qtd. and tr. Birley, Marcus Aurelius, 94.

Ad Marcum Caesarem 4.3, qtd. and tr. Birley, Marcus Aurelius, 69.

De Eloquentia 4.5 (= Haines 2.74), qtd. and tr. Birley, Marcus Aurelius, 95. Alan Cameron, in his review of Birley's biography (The Classical Review 17:3 (1967): 347), suggests a reference to chapter 11 of Arthur Darby Nock's Conversion (Oxford: Oxford University Press, 1933, rept. 1961): "Conversion to Philosophy".

Birley, Marcus Aurelius, 94, 105.

Birley, Marcus Aurelius, 95; Champlin, Fronto, 120.

Champlin, Fronto, 174 n. 12.

Ad Antoninum Imperator 1.2.2 (= Haines 2.36), qtd. and tr. Birley, Marcus Aurelius, 95.

Birley, Marcus Aurelius, 94–95, 101.

Champlin, Fronto, 120.

Meditations 1.7, qtd. and tr. Birley, Marcus Aurelius, 94–95.

Birley, Marcus Aurelius, 103.

Ad Marcum Caesarem 4.11 (= Haines 1.202ff), qtd. and tr. Birley, Marcus Aurelius, 105.

Birley, Marcus Aurelius, 247 F.1.

Birley, Marcus Aurelius, 206–07.

Meditations 9.40, qtd. and tr. Birley, Marcus Aurelius, 207.

Meditations 10.34, tr. Farquharson, 78, 224.

Birley, Marcus Aurelius, 107.

Birley, Marcus Aurelius, 107–08.

Birley, Marcus Aurelius, 108.

Inscriptiones Graecae ad Res Romanas pertinentes 4.1399, qtd. and tr. Birley, Marcus Aurelius, 114.

Birley, Marcus Aurelius, 114.

Reed, 194.

Lendering, "Marcus Aurelius".

HA Verus 2.9–11; 3.4–7; Birley, Marcus Aurelius, 108.

Suetonius, Nero 6.1; HA Verus 1.8; Barnes, "Hadrian and Lucius Verus", 67; Birley, Marcus Aurelius, 158.

See also: Barnes, "Hadrian and Lucius Verus", 69–70;

Pierre Lambrechts, "L'empereur Lucius Verus. Essai de réhabilitation" (in French), Antiquité Classique 3 (1934), 173ff.

Barnes, "Hadrian and Lucius Verus", 66. Poorly compiled: e.g. Barnes, "Hadrian and Lucius Verus", 68.

Barnes, "Hadrian and Lucius Verus", 68–69.

HA Verus 2.9-11; 3.4-7; Barnes, "Hadrian and Lucius Verus", 68; Birley, Marcus Aurelius, 108.

Birley, Marcus Aurelius, 112.

Bowman, 156; Victor, 15:7

Victor, 15:7

Dio 71.33.4–5; Birley, Marcus Aurelius, 114.

Bury, 532.

HA Antoninus Pius 12.4–8; Birley, Marcus Aurelius, 114.

Bowman, 156.

HA Marcus 7.5, qtd. and tr. Birley, Marcus Aurelius, 116.

Birley, Marcus Aurelius, 116. Birley takes the phrase horror imperii from HA Pert. 13.1 and 15.8.

Birley, "Hadrian to the Antonines", 156.

HA Verus 3.8; Birley, Marcus Aurelius, 116; "Hadrian to the Antonines", 156.

HA Verus 4.1; Marcus 7.5; Birley, Marcus Aurelius, 116.

Birley, Marcus Aurelius, 116–17.

Birley, Marcus Aurelius, 117; "Hadrian to the Antonines", 157 n.53.

Birley, "Hadrian to the Antonines", 157 n.53.

Birley, Marcus Aurelius, 117.

HA Verus 4.2, tr. David Magie, cited in Birley, Marcus Aurelius, 117, 278 n.4.

HA Marcus 7.9; Verus 4.3; Birley, Marcus Aurelius, 117–18.

HA Marcus 7.9; Verus 4.3; Birley, Marcus Aurelius, 117–18. "twice the size": Duncan-Jones, 109.

Birley, Marcus Aurelius, 118.

Roman Currency of the Principate.

HA Marcus 7.10, tr. David Magie, cited in Birley, Marcus Aurelius, 118, 278 n.6.

HA Marcus 7.10–11; Birley, Marcus Aurelius, 118.

HA Antoninus Pius 12.8; Birley, Marcus Aurelius, 118–19.

HA Marcus 7.4; Birley, Marcus Aurelius, 119.

HA Comm. 1.3; Birley, Marcus Aurelius, 119.

HA Comm. 1.2; Birley, Marcus Aurelius, 119.

HA Marcus 19.1–2; Birley, Marcus Aurelius, 278 n.9.

HA Comm. 1.4, 10.2; Birley, Marcus Aurelius, 119.

Birley, Marcus Aurelius, 119, citing H. Mattingly, Coins of the Roman Empire in the British Museum IV: Antoninus Pius to Commodus (London, 1940), Marcus Aurelius and Lucius Verus, nos. 155ff.; 949ff.

HA Marcus 7.7; Birley, Marcus Aurelius, 118.

Birley, Marcus Aurelius, 118, citing Werner Eck, Die Organization Italiens (1979), 146ff.

HA Marcus 8.1, qtd. and tr. Birley, Marcus Aurelius, 119; "Hadrian to the Antonines", 157.

Birley, Marcus Aurelius, 122–23, citing H.G. Pfalum,

Les carrières procuratoriennes équestres sous le Haut-Empire romain I–III (Paris, 1960–61); Supplément (Paris, 1982), nos. 142; 156; Eric Birley, Roman Britain and the Roman Army (1953), 142ff., 151ff.

Birley, Marcus Aurelius, 123, citing H.G. Pfalum, Les carrières procuratoriennes équestres sous le Haut-Empire romain I–III (Paris, 1960–61); Supplément (Paris, 1982), no. 141.

HA Marcus 8.8; Birley, Marcus Aurelius, 123, citing W. Eck, Die Satthalter der germ. Provinzen (1985), 65ff.

Birley, Marcus Aurelius, 120, citing Ad Verum Imperator 1.3.2 (= Haines 1.298ff).

Ad Antoninum Imperator 4.2.3 (= Haines 1.302ff), qtd. and tr. Birley, Marcus Aurelius, 119.

Birley, Marcus Aurelius, 120.

Birley, Marcus Aurelius, 120, citing Ad Verum Imperator 1.1 (= Haines 1.305).

Ad Antoninum Imperator 4.1 (= Haines 1.300ff), qtd. and tr. Birley, Marcus Aurelius, 120.

HA Marcus 8.3–4; Birley, Marcus Aurelius, 120.

Birley, Marcus Aurelius, 120, citing H. Mattingly, Coins of the Roman Empire in the British Museum IV: Antoninus Pius to Commodus (London, 1940), Marcus Aurelius and Lucius Verus, nos. 841; 845.

Gregory S. Aldrete, Floods of the Tiber in ancient Rome (Baltimore: Johns Hopkins University Press, 2007), 30–31.

HA Marcus 8.4–5; Birley, Marcus Aurelius, 120.

Inscriptiones Latinae Selectae 5932 (Nepos), 1092

(Priscus); Birley, Marcus Aurelius, 121.

HA Marcus 11.3, cited in Birley, Marcus Aurelius, 278 n.16.

Ad Antoninum Imperator 1.2.2 (= Haines 2.35), qtd. and tr. Birley, Marcus Aurelius, 128.

De eloquentia 1.12 (= Haines 2.63–65), qtd. and tr. Birley, Marcus Aurelius, 128.

Ad Antoninum Imperator 1.2.2 (= Haines 2.35); Birley, Marcus Aurelius, 127–28.

Ad Antoninum Imperator 1.2.4 (= Haines 2.41–43), tr. Haines; Birley, Marcus Aurelius, 128.

HA Antoninus Pius 12.7; Birley, Marcus Aurelius, 114, 121.

Event: HA Marcus 8.6; Birley, Marcus Aurelius, 121. Date: Jaap-Jan Flinterman, "The Date of Lucian's Visit to Abonuteichos," Zeitschrift für Papyrologie und Epigraphik 119 (1997): 281.

HA Marcus 8.6; Birley, Marcus Aurelius, 121.

Lucian, Alexander 27; Birley, Marcus Aurelius, 121.

Lucian, Alexander 27; Birley, Marcus Aurelius, 121–22. On Alexander, see: Robin Lane Fox, Pagans and Christians (Harmondsworth: Penguin, 1986), 241–50.

Birley, Marcus Aurelius, 278 n.19.

Dio 71.2.1; Lucian, Historia Quomodo Conscribenda 21, 24, 25; Birley, Marcus Aurelius, 121–22.

HA Marcus 8.7; Birley, Marcus Aurelius, 122.

HA Antoninus Pius 7.11; Marcus 7.2; Birley, Marcus Aurelius, 103–04, 122.

Pan. Ath. 203–04, qtd. and tr. Alan Cameron, review

of Anthony Birley's Marcus Aurelius, The Classical Review 17:3 (1967): 349.

HA Marcus 8.6; Birley, Marcus Aurelius, 123.

Corpus Inscriptionum Latinarum 8.7050-51; Birley, Marcus Aurelius, 123.

Incriptiones Latinae Selectae 1097-98; Birley, Marcus Aurelius, 123.

Incriptiones Latinae Selectae 1091; Birley, Marcus Aurelius, 123.

Incriptiones Latinae Selectae 2311; Birley, Marcus Aurelius, 123.

HA Marcus 12.13; Birley, Marcus Aurelius, 123.

L'Année Épigraphique 1972.657 Archived 29 April 2012 at the Wayback Machine.; Birley, Marcus Aurelius, 125.

HA Verus 9.2; Birley, Marcus Aurelius, 125.

De Feriis Alsiensibus 1 (= Haines 2.3); Birley, Marcus Aurelius, 126.

De Feriis Alsiensibus 3.1 (= Haines 2.5), qtd. and tr. Birley, Marcus Aurelius, 126.

De Feriis Alsiensibus 3.4 (= Haines 2.9); Birley, Marcus Aurelius, 126-27.

De Feriis Alsiensibus 3.6-12 (= Haines 2.11-19); Birley, Marcus Aurelius, 126-27.

De Feriis Alsiensibus 4, tr. Haines 2.19; Birley, Marcus Aurelius, 127.

De Feriis Alsiensibus 4 (= Haines 2.19), qtd. and tr. Birley, Marcus Aurelius, 127.

Ad Verum Imperator 2.1.19 (= Haines 2.149); Birley,

Marcus Aurelius, 129.

De bello Parthico 10 (= Haines 2.31), qtd. and tr. Birley, Marcus Aurelius, 127.

De bello Parthico 1-2 (= Haines 2.21-23).

De bello Parthico 1 (= Haines 2.21), qtd. and tr. Birley, Marcus Aurelius, 127.

Dio 71.1.3; Birley, Marcus Aurelius, 123.

HA Verus 5.8; Birley, Marcus Aurelius, 123, 125.

Birley, Marcus Aurelius, 125.

HA Marcus 8.9, tr. Magie; Birley, Marcus Aurelius, 123-26. On Lucius' voyage, see: HA Verus 6.7-9; HA Marcus 8.10-11; Birley, Marcus Aurelius, 125-26.

Birley, Marcus Aurelius, 129.

HA Verus 4.4; Birley, Marcus Aurelius, 129.

HA Verus 4.6, tr. Magie; cf. 5.7; Birley, Marcus Aurelius, 129.

HA Verus 8.7, 8.10-11; Fronto, Principae Historia 17 (= Haines 2.217); Birley, Marcus Aurelius, 129.

Barnes, 69.

HA Verus 9.2; Corpus Inscriptionum Latinarum 3.199 Archived 29 April 2012 at the Wayback Machine.; Birley, Marcus Aurelius, 130-31.

HA Verus 7.7; Marcus 9.4; Barnes, 72; Birley, "Hadrian to the Antonines", 163; cf. also Barnes, "Legislation Against the Christians", 39; "Some Persons in the Historia Augusta", 142, citing the Vita Abercii 44ff.

HA Verus 7.10; Lucian, Imagines 3; Birley, Marcus Aurelius, 131. Cf. Lucian, Imagines, Pro Imaginibus, passim.

Birley, Marcus Aurelius, 131; "Hadrian to the Antonines", 163.

HA Verus 7.7; Marcus 9.4; Birley, Marcus Aurelius, 131.

Birley, Marcus Aurelius, 131, citing Anné Épigraphique 1958.15.

HA Verus 7.7; Birley, Marcus Aurelius, 131.

HA Marcus 9.4; Birley, Marcus Aurelius, 131.

HA Marcus 9.5–6; Birley, Marcus Aurelius, 131.

HA Marcus 9.1; Birley, "Hadrian to the Antonines", 162.

HA Marcus 9.1; HA Verus 7.1–2; Ad Verrum Imperator 2.3 (= Haines 2.133); Birley, Marcus Aurelius, 129; "Hadrian to the Antonines", 162.

Birley, Marcus Aurelius, 129; "Hadrian to the Antonines", 162, citing H. Mattingly, Coins of the Roman Empire in the British Museum IV: Antoninus Pius to Commodus (London, 1940), Marcus Aurelius and Lucius Verus, nos. 233ff.

Dio 71.3.1; Birley, Marcus Aurelius, 131; "Hadrian to the Antonines", 162; Millar, Near East, 113.

Birley, Marcus Aurelius, 280 n. 42; "Hadrian to the Antonines", 162.

Birley, Marcus Aurelius, 131; "Hadrian to the Antonines", 162, citing H. Mattingly, Coins of the Roman Empire in the British Museum IV: Antoninus Pius to Commodus (London, 1940), Marcus Aurelius and Lucius Verus, nos. 261ff.; 300 ff.

Birley, Marcus Aurelius, 130, 279 n. 38; "Hadrian to

the Antonines", 163, citing Prosopographia Imperii Romani2 M 169; Millar, Near East, 112.

Birley, Marcus Aurelius, 130; "Hadrian to the Antonines", 162.

Fronto, Ad Verum Imperator 2.1.3 (= Haines 2.133); Astarita, 41; Birley, Marcus Aurelius, 130; "Hadrian to the Antonines", 162.

Inscriptiones Latinae Selectae 1098; Birley, Marcus Aurelius, 130.

Birley, "Hadrian to the Antonines", 163, citing Prosopographia Imperii Romani2 M 169.

Lucian, Historia Quomodo Conscribenda 15, 19; Birley, "Hadrian to the Antonines", 163.

Lucian, Historia Quomodo Conscribenda 20, 28; Birley, "Hadrian to the Antonines", 163, citing Syme, Roman Papers, 5.689ff.

HA Verus 8.3–4; Birley, "Hadrian to the Antonines", 163. Birley cites R.H. McDowell, Coins from Seleucia on the Tigris (Ann Arbor: University of Michigan Press, 1935), 124ff., on the date.

Birley, "Hadrian to the Antonines", 164.

Birley, "Hadrian to the Antonines", 164, citing H. Mattingly, Coins of the Roman Empire in the British Museum IV: Antoninus Pius to Commodus (London, 1940), Marcus Aurelius and Lucius Verus, nos. 384 ff., 1248 ff., 1271 ff.

Birley, "Hadrian to the Antonines", 164, citing P. Kneissl, Die Siegestitulatur der römischen Kaiser. Untersuchungen zu den Siegerbeinamen des 1. und 2.

Jahrhunderts (Göttingen, 1969), 99 ff.

Birley, "Hadrian to the Antonines", 164, citing H. Mattingly, Coins of the Roman Empire in the British Museum IV: Antoninus Pius to Commodus (London, 1940), Marcus Aurelius and Lucius Verus, nos. 401ff.

Birley, Marcus Aurelius, 253.

Birley, Marcus Aurelius, 183.

Dio 72.11.3–4; Ad amicos 1.12 (= Haines 2.173); Birley, Marcus Aurelius, 132.

Dio 72.11.3–4; Birley, Marcus Aurelius, 132, citing De nepote amisso 2 (= Haines 2.222); Ad Verum Imperator 2.9–10 (= Haines 2.232ff.).

Birley, Marcus Aurelius, 133, citing Geza Alföldy, Konsulat und Senatorenstand (1977), Moesia Inferior: 232 f.; Moesia Superior: 234f.; Pannonia Superior: 236f.; Dacia: 245f.; Pannonia Inferior: 251.

McLynn, Marcus Aurelius: A Life, 323–24.

Le Bohec, 56.

Grant, The Antonines: The Roman Empire in Transition, 29.

Dio 72.11.4-5; Birley, Marcus Aurelius, 253.

Fergus Millar, The Emperor in the Roman World, 31 BC – AD 337 (London: Duckworth, 1977), 6 and passim. See also: idem. "Emperors at Work", Journal of Roman Studies 57:1/2 (1967): 9–19.

Thinkers at War. "Pius, one of longest-serving emperors, became infirm in his last years, so Marcus Aurelius gradually assumed the imperial duties. By the time he succeeded in AD 161, he was already well-practised in public administration."

Codex Justinianus 7.2.6, qtd. and tr. Birley, Marcus Aurelius, 133.

Digest 31.67.10, qtd. and tr. Birley, Marcus Aurelius, 133.

Birley, Marcus Aurelius, 133.

William b. Irvine, A Guide to the Good Life: The Ancient Art of Stoic Joy, Oxford University Press, 2009, pp.57-58

Cassius Dio, 72.33

Pulleyblank, Leslie and Gardiner, 71–79.

Yü, 460–61.

De Crespigny, 600.

An, 83.

Young, 29–30.

For further information on Óc Eo, see Osborne, Milton. The Mekong: Turbulent Past, Uncertain Future. Crows Nest: Allen & Unwin, 2006, revised edition, first published in 2000. pp. 24–25. ISBN 9781741148930.

Ball, 154.

Haeser, 24–33.

"There is not enough evidence satisfactorily to identify the disease or diseases" concluded J. F. Gilliam in his summary (1961) of the written sources, with inconclusive Greek and Latin inscriptions, two groups of papyri and coinage.

Dio Cassius, LXXII 14.3–4; his book that would cover the plague under Marcus is missing; this later outburst was the greatest of which the historian had knowledge.

Murphy.

Plague in the Ancient World.

Kleiner, 230.

Merrony, 85.

Birley, "Hadrian to the Antonines", 186–91.

Tr. Cary, ad loc.

Cassius Dio 72.36, 72.34

Grant, The Climax Of Rome, 15.

HA Marcus 1.1, 27.7; Dio 71.1.1; James Francis, Subversive Virtue: Asceticism and Authority in the Second-Century Pagan World (University Park: Pennsylvania State University Press, 1995), 21 n. 1.

Mark.

Francis, 21 n.1, citing Justin, 1 Apologia 1; Athenagoras, Leg. 1; Eusebius, Historia Ecclesiastica 4.26.9–11.

Eusebius, Historia Ecclesiastica 4.26.9–11, qtd. and tr. Francis, 21 n. 1.

Herodian, Ab Excessu Divi Marci 1.2.4, tr. Echols.

Thinkers at War.

Barnes, "Legislation Against the Christians".

McLynn, Marcus Aurelius: A Life, 295.

Gibbon, Ch. 16 Pt. 5.

Stephens, 31.

Lendering, "Antoninus and Aelius".

Ackermann, Schroeder, Terry, Lo Upshur and Whitters, 39.

McLynn, Marcus Aurelius: A Life, 92.

Stertz, 434, citing Themistius, Oratio 6.81; HA Cassius 3.5; Aurelius Victor, De Caesaribus 16.9.

Hays, xlviii–xlix.

Hadot, 22.

Equestrian Statue of Marcus Aurelius.

Kleiner, 193.

Printed in Great Britain
by Amazon

59625957R00187